# What America Can Learn From Israel

# DAVID RUBIN

**Shiloh**
**ISRAEL**Press

**Confronting Radicals:**
**What America Can Learn From Israel**
ISBN 978-1-7362016-0-2

Published by Shiloh Israel Press
Copyright © 2021 by David Rubin

www.DavidRubinIsrael.com
www.ShilohIsraelChildren.org
www.Facebook.com/DavidRubin.Shiloh.Israel

*Contact The Author*
David@ShilohIsraelChildren.org
1-845-738-1522

*Contact The Publisher*
sipress@ShilohIsraelChildren.org

*For Orders*
1-800-431-1579 (toll-free)

*Book Development and Cover Design*
Chaim Mazo – chaim.mazo@gmail.com

*Cover Layout*
Christopher Tobias

Printed in The United States Of America

*This book is dedicated to the memory of two distinguished individuals:*

*British writer George Orwell*
*and*
*US Senator Daniel Patrick Moynihan*

*While residing on two different continents in two different generations, both of these men were thinkers, who were not afraid to tell the truth and to point out falsehood.*

*In our generation, more such bold thinkers are needed, with the courage to think beyond "political correctness" and to fearlessly express their thoughts. This is especially urgent today, because of the growing cadre of radical thought police who tell Americans what they can and can't say, who change the meanings of words, and most nefariously, attempt to rewrite history.*

*As Orwell would say, "If liberty means anything at all, it means the right to tell people what they do not want to hear."*

# Contents

"The riots and the looting of the radical Left that have engulfed and terrorized many American cities periodically in recent years seemed to reach unprecedented levels in 2020, continuing into 2021, and have heightened the polarization in our country. The mob scenes that were called 'protests' were ostensibly about police racism, but the reality was quite different. Those who peacefully protest genuine racism don't burn American flags, don't vandalize monuments to American heroes, and don't burn Bibles. In *Confronting Radicals: What America Can Learn from Israel*, David Rubin illustrates frightening parallels to Israel's struggles combatting Palestinian terrorism and the radical Muslim propaganda machine. By learning from Israel's many successes, as well as its many mistakes, we begin to understand that when confronting radicals, appeasement and willful ignorance don't work. Rubin has written a powerful guidebook for these difficult times."

**David Webb** – *Fox Nation Host, Fox News Contributor, The Hill Columnist, and SiriusXM Patriot Host*

"The United States and Israel are two countries that are bonded together, based on eternal Biblical values that have stood the test of time. Those values that America's Founders so admired are under assault today by secular radicals who abhor the great Judeo-Christian heritage that made America the envy of the world. Meanwhile, on the other side of the globe, the embattled nation of

Israel continues to be a light unto the nations. After enduring horrific slavery in Egypt, ancient Israel thrived in the glory days of King David and King Solomon, but later suffered from exiles, persecutions, and mass slaughter, before the miraculous rise of the modern State of Israel. Despite that adversity, or perhaps because of it, the Israeli experience is a valuable resource that we can all learn from. In *Confronting Radicals: What America Can Learn from Israel*, David Rubin addresses the political and cultural turmoil in America and provides an action plan from Israel to counter the radicals and to restore American exceptionalism. His compelling words from Zion should be heeded!"

**Chris Mitchell** – *Middle East Bureau Chief, CBN News*

"*Confronting Radicals: What America Can Learn from Israel* sheds much needed light on the false allure of the socialist revolution that is rising in America. David Rubin calls to action Americans who are willing to fight for their country's values and to push back against the impending 'Orwellian' future where our thoughts, words, and actions are controlled and cancelled."

**Mike Huckabee** – *Former Arkansas governor, political commentator on Fox News Channel, TBN, and Newsmax TV*

"There are many well-meaning liberals who shout out slogans like 'Black Lives Matter', thinking that they are fighting for social justice. Rabbi Abraham Joshua Heschel famously marched in peace alongside Martin Luther King Jr. in the 1960s, but so much has changed since then. The radical leftists of today are marching to the beat of a different drummer, not advocating for peaceful change that respects and honors America's great heritage, but actually, are seeking to tear it down, both physically and spiritually. Author David Rubin has brought us valuable lessons from Israel's rich Biblical and modern heritage, including its valiant effort to confront political propaganda and terrorism from the radical Palestinian movement. Last, but certainly not least, Rubin describes the magnificent Jewish focus on family and education, which encouraged the remarkable, enterprising spirit that enabled poor Jewish immigrants to achieve great success in America. *Confronting Radicals: What America Can Learn from Israel* is the Jewish guidebook for this very politically involved generation. I strongly endorse its message!"

**Rabbi Dov Peretz Elkins** – *Co-Author, Chicken Soup for the Jewish Soul*

"David Rubin's book, *Confronting Radicals: What America Can Learn from Israel*, is vital to preserving Western Civilization. Leviticus 19:17 states: 'Confront people directly so you will not be held guilty for their sin.' Radicals have become experts in psychological projection, or blame-shifting, in which they accuse you of what they are guilty of. Peaceable people find it uncomfortable and out of character to stand up against injustice, but what is the consequence if they do not? Our children will grow up under tyranny! Proverbs 13:22 admonishes: 'A good man leaves an inheritance to his children's children.' Rubin reveals in his book how peace-loving citizens in America can skillfully and knowledgeably defend their families and future, but that requires courage. Dietrich Bonhoeffer, who resisted Hitler, once warned: 'Silence in the face of evil is itself evil: God will not hold us guiltless.' The plan of the radical, secular Left to uproot the foundation of American exceptionalism from its noble roots must be confronted, and it must be done so in all of the peaceful, yet determined ways described in this extraordinary piece of work. I highly recommend David Rubin's insightful and inspiring book, a must read for every freedom-loving citizen."

**William J. Federer** – *Historian, best-selling author, and nationally known speaker*

"Radical, violent groups like BLM and Antifa in America, and radical Palestinian terror groups like Hamas and Fatah in Israel, have long used similar tactics, and indeed, promote a similar strategy of low-level terrorism, as a means to create anarchy and do maximum damage to the lives of ordinary citizens. In fact, the collusion between the radical Left and radical Islam, while surprising to some, actually makes a lot of sense. Their long-term visions of government are sharply different, but their immediate goals of creating anarchy and fear in countries that cherish freedom are shockingly similar. In *Confronting Radicals: What America Can Learn from Israel*, David Rubin has provided us with the full picture, exposing the multi-faceted assault on America and how it can be defeated. This book is a must read for the survival of Judeo-Christian civilization!"

**Robert Spencer** – *Director of Jihad Watch (David Horowitz Freedom Center), New York Times best-selling author*

# The Author

David Rubin is a former mayor of Shiloh, Israel – in the region of Samaria, which together with Judea, is known to much of the world as the West Bank. He is founder and president of Shiloh Israel Children's Fund (SICF) – dedicated to healing the trauma of child victims of terrorist attacks, as well as rebuilding the Biblical heartland of Israel through the children. SICF was established after Rubin and his three-year-old son were wounded in a vicious terrorist shooting attack, as they were driving home from Jerusalem. Bleeding profusely in a car that wouldn't start, they barely managed to escape as the bullets were flying.

Rubin vowed to retaliate – not with hatred, nor with anger, but with compassion – to create positive change for Israel and its children. SICF sustains a unique therapeutic-educational campus for 2,000 children who have been negatively impacted by the ongoing terrorist attacks targeting Israeli civilians.

David Rubin has written seven books. In addition to his latest, *Confronting Radicals: What America Can Learn from Israel*, he is also the author of *God, Israel, & Shiloh, The Islamic Tsunami, Peace for Peace*, and, most recently, *Trump and the Jews*, which pierced through the media turmoil surrounding President Donald Trump to examine his warm relationship with Israel and his complex relationship with American Jews.

Rubin appears as a frequent commentator on Fox News, Newsmax TV, One America News, and many other television and radio networks, while his articles have appeared in Israel National News (Arutz Sheva), Jerusalem Post, US News and World Report, and numerous other publications.

A featured speaker throughout North America and elsewhere, Rubin has been called "The Trusted Voice of Israel."

Born and raised in Brooklyn, Rubin resides in Israel with his wife and children on a hilltop overlooking the site of Ancient Shiloh, the hallowed ground where the Tabernacle of Israel stood for three hundred and sixty-nine years, in the time of Joshua, Hannah, and Samuel the Prophet.

# Introduction

Orwell's classic, "1984" foresaw a terribly frightening scenario of how tyranny breeds tyranny, but at the time his book was written, few Americans thought that such a prescient vision could be referring to the United States of America, the land of the free and the home of the brave.

Indeed, the recent images of great American cities in flames and even transformed, at least temporarily, into boarded up ghost towns, have been shocking, but they can only be truly understood when one looks at the full picture, in order to see how an assortment of events and processes, joined together in a not so spontaneous convergence, are threatening the great American civilization like never before.

These troubling occurrences have included the recurring riots and looting, the domestic terrorism that has shocked millions of Americans, the intense identity politics being played by a major American political party that has repeatedly pandered to the radical Left in recent years, the culture war led by the "cancel culture" that attempts to shut down and censor any voices that express opposition to the leftist elites, and the premeditated effort to politically, socially, and economically transform America.

This radical plan, which has been gradually actualized in recent decades, would change the United States from a nation that believes in the traditional values of God, family, and hard work, to a new Marxist, gender-confused, ethnically-confused reality that sees the United

States as an evil force in the world.

We are not talking about a spontaneous protest movement. When former first lady Michelle Obama said that the election of her husband marked the first time that she was proud of America, that should have been a warning sign. [1]

When her husband strangely told Charles Bolden, the head of NASA, that one of his top priorities should be to "find a way to reach out to the Muslim world and engage much more with predominantly Muslim nations to help them feel good about their historic contribution to science, math and engineering," [2] that, too, should have been a warning sign.

Jumping ahead a few years, we saw the emergence of the Occupy Wall Street protest movement in 2011, which created havoc in the streets of New York City and many other American cities with its wild behavior in support of a vague, yet resolutely anti-capitalist agenda. Those demonstrations quickly spread, and there, as well, the signs of future danger should have been noted. [3]

In January of 2017, violent street protests and vandalism were the response to Donald J. Trump's surprising, yet decisive victory in a free and fair presidential election. Unlike the 2020 election, there were no legal claims of election fraud. The results were not being disputed, not in the courts nor through any other legitimate channels, yet the violent rioters seemed to be saying that Trump did not have a right to win fair and square. One could not avoid observing the rage in the eyes of the many rioters who smashed store windows and the windows of government buildings in the nation's capital on an Inauguration Day that should have been, whatever one's political opinions, a celebration of the

American political process and an orderly, magnanimous transition. [4]

Sadly, we are not talking about peaceful protest in the hope of achieving dialogue, tolerance, and mutual respect. We are talking about an Orwellian revolution in which differing opinions are stifled and thoughts controlled, and it seems increasingly clear that a growing number of Americans are very concerned.

In a recent survey, it was revealed that 61% of Americans believe that the United States is heading towards a second civil war, including a shocking 41% who "strongly agree" with that assessment. [5] More than half are already stockpiling food and other essential items to survive and fight back.

Whether we call it a civil war, or more accurately, a radical leftist revolution, the process is definitely in motion. While the Covid-19 pandemic probably heightened the anger and the feelings of desperation and polarization on both sides, the sparks leading to revolution have been igniting for many years, probably since the 1960s, when the lofty brotherhood and sisterhood sentiments, coupled with the good-feeling music of peace and love, were quickly overtaken by the radical, angry, socialist ideologues who had an unabashed political, social, and economic agenda. Even though it seemed that many of those ideologues joined the establishment in the 1970s, which many of them actually did, their passion for radicalism simply went underground temporarily and now it is bursting forth in all of its dubious glory, with many of those former street radicals financing the budding revolution from their own corporate boardrooms.

Several key questions, out of many, that demand

answers: How did America get to this point? Weren't the recent protests all about anti-racism and stopping police brutality? Could it be an overreaction to call it a revolution? Last, but not least, why is this book being written by an Israeli?

Well, actually an American-Israeli. I was born and raised in New York's outer borough of Brooklyn, in a time of rising crime and racial tension. During those days, I loved playing basketball in the local park. On the court, there was no such thing as racism, but in my high school, in which there was forced integration, with some 35% of students bussed in from the black slums, you could cut the tension with a very sharp knife. Speaking of knives, I was mugged twice as a teenager by black thugs, once at knifepoint and once at gunpoint. Similarly, my father, who was also a teacher, was robbed at gunpoint while supervising a school lunchroom. Several years later, as a young adult, I experienced racism (and anti-Semitism), while teaching in an inner-city public school. The black principal would openly express her hatred of white people, and specifically, Jews. Together with her Black Muslim social worker sidekick, she methodically harassed and worked to push out the few white teachers that remained in the school. While I knew enough about the history of racism to know about slavery and the civil rights movement, these personal experiences revealed to me that racism can go both ways.

Moving to Israel some thirty years ago, I came to an ancient country filled with its returning Jews of many races and ethnic backgrounds, some of whom trace their recent roots to a wide variety of countries like Morocco, Yemen, Russia, the United States, India, Ethiopia, China, France, and Mexico. Israel is, indeed, a unique country, with unique people, who have escaped persecution, discrimination, and mass slaughter to rebuild their ancient homeland. The varied experiences of a people that was scattered around the world for almost two thousand years and have returned to rebuild are a vast resource that everyone can learn from, especially our American friends in these challenging times.

It says in the Jewish guidebook, the Torah, or more specifically, the writings of the Prophets, that we are to be "a light unto the nations." The learning that can be weaned from our example and experience can be derived from our numerous successes, but also from our mistakes, and we have had many of those, as well.

Israel is the country that I have chosen to live in for positive reasons, not for any negative reasons having to do with my country of birth. I have sacrificed a lot to live here and was even wounded some years ago, in an attack by Muslim terrorists, along with my then three-year-old son, who was shot in the head. I love Israel with every fiber of my being, yet I remain a proud dual citizen.

The United States is a great, but troubled country with a rich history that all of its citizens should be proud of, even if there have been many ups and downs, and a lot of badly needed corrections made along the way. Life is complicated and always needs to be understood in historical context. My hope is that by studying the recent events in the United States and comparing them to the Israeli/Jewish experience, my beloved country of birth will discover some of the necessary solutions to meet the challenges, and hopefully will succeed in preventing the radical revolution that wants to transform America from a beacon of light for a declining Judeo-Christian civilization, to a confused intolerant caricature of a

Socialist utopia that has never existed.

That is the radical Left's social agenda, and it has been moving forward, methodically and strategically, for several decades and on many fronts. Despite the Trump presidency, which reversed some of the political excesses of the Obama years, the leftist social and educational agenda has progressed almost unimpeded at the local level. Conservatives have watched helplessly as states like Georgia seemed to somehow turn Democrat overnight.

On January 6, 2021, in Washington, DC, there was a backlash from the right that shocked the world, as an overflow pro-Trump rally protesting alleged electoral fraud marched into the Capitol building, some peacefully, but some not, and it soon became a brawl. While it's true that there was a radical Left and neo-Nazi presence in the crowd inciting violence, [6] the infiltration was unacceptable in any event. The lawlessness in the Capitol was terrible, with some tragic results.

However, it must be emphasized that the disturbances in the Capitol paled in comparison to the hundreds of riots of the radical Left just in 2020 alone (and they have continued well into 2021), the insurrectional nature of which has been totally ignored by most of the mainstream media. Suddenly, after the tragic events in the Capitol, the media discovered words like "insurrection" that had been left unspoken for an entire year. This, despite the fact that during the Left's numerous demonstrations of rioting, looting, destruction, and death, police had been spit upon, verbally abused, physically attacked, and murdered. In addition to that, monuments to American heroes throughout the country were vandalized and knocked down, all in the name of "social justice." What the one-day "response" in the Capitol reminded us of is that another civil war is indeed a possibility, and that this should greatly concern everyone.

That being said, every American should remember that the terrible events in the Capitol, were a brief reaction to years of abuse from a radical Left that has sought to dismantle the magnificent system of values that made America great. Those values, most of which were based on Judeo-Christian civilization, made the USA the country that people from around the world have flocked to and admired.

However, we must remember that a country that abandons its roots and its foundations is bound to eventually collapse. The ancient nation of Israel learned that sad lesson from its two painful exiles and from the struggles of its modern rebirth. Perhaps some valuable lessons from Israel's successes, as well as its mistakes, can help to slow down and even halt America's frightening process of societal self-destruction. Hopefully, by learning lessons from history, America's process of decline can be reversed.

*Chapter One*
# The Israel-US Connection

*"I had faith in Israel before it was established, I have faith in it now … I believe it has a glorious future before it – not just another sovereign nation, but as an embodiment of the great ideals of our civilization."*

(President Harry S. Truman – May 1948) [1]

Israelis are a proud people. They are proud of their unique history and their savvy survival skills. Those Israelis who are religiously or Biblically connected see the hand of God in their amazing return to the Land of Israel as a sovereign nation again after approximately 1,900 years of exile. During two millennia as a dispersed people scattered around the world, the Jews suffered persecution, discrimination, and genocide on a scale previously unknown to western civilization, but the Jewish response to adversity was not to call for "Days of Rage," nor to make demands of those who may have wronged them. The Jewish response was never to riot, nor to rebel, and never to disrespect the laws of their host countries through violent looting, assault on police officers, nor the defacing of national monuments, as has been witnessed recently in the United States of America.

The many centuries of difficult exile and dispersion would have broken a less resilient people, and perhaps could have caused them to lash out with anger, but the Jewish reaction was qualitatively different and intrinsically positive by nature, an approach to life that was rooted in the teachings of Torah wisdom.

**Slavery in Egypt:** "The Egyptians enslaved the Children of Israel with crushing harshness. They embittered their lives with brutal work, with mortar and with bricks and with every labor of the field…" (Exodus 1:13-14)

*"The purely righteous do not complain of the dark, but increase the light; they do not complain of evil, but increase justice; they do not complain of heresy, but increase faith; they do not complain of ignorance, but increase wisdom."*

(Rabbi Avraham Yitzhak Kook) [2]

**Seeing the Good in Everyone:** Rabbi Avraham Yitzhak Kook, the first chief rabbi of the Land of Israel, was known not just for his vast knowledge of Torah, but for his ability to focus on the good in everyone and to bring out the best by emphasizing the positive.

In practice, Jews have learned to be creative, industrious, and to cling to their heritage, because without that, they would have, despite all of their accomplishments, been eaten up by the often hostile locals in the lands in which they dwelled. More to the point, they would not have accomplished a fraction of what they have accomplished without an attitude that understands and learns from the past but focuses on living productive lives in the present, and ultimately, in the future. Jews have, in most cases, learned valuable lessons from the horrible events in their past, including the worst of them, such as the painful history as slaves in Egypt some three thousand three hundred years ago and, more recently, the slaughter of six million Jews in the Nazi Holocaust, but never allowed these events to prevent them from moving forward.

*"We cannot choose our external circumstances, but we can always choose how we respond to them."*

(Epictetus, Greek Philosopher) [3]

Yes, the Jewish people have overcome great adversity, have survived, and thrived, despite everything; and have reestablished their nation again in the same land that the

Bible speaks of repeatedly.

*"And God told Abraham … Raise now your eyes and look out from where you are: northward, southward, eastward, and westward. For all the land that you see, to you will I give it, and to your descendants forever."*

(Genesis 13: 14-15)

Zionism is the movement of the Jewish people to return to the Land of Israel as a sovereign nation again in our times. The process of return, which began in the late nineteenth century, continued with the establishment of the State of Israel in 1948, and has continued ever since. It happened with the consent of the League of Nations in 1917, the San Remo Conference in 1920, and eventually the United Nations in 1947, but most of the work was accomplished through the sweat and self-sacrifice of Jewish pioneers and with three rag-tag militias that rebelled against the British colonial authority that refused to grant Israel independence.

With great self-sacrifice, Jewish farmers fertilized a seemingly barren land with no apparent natural resources, all the while surrounded by an Arab population that was hostile to the return of Jewish sovereignty in what had become an Islamic-dominated Middle East.

Nonetheless, despite decades of Arab-initiated wars and ongoing terrorism against its civilian population, Israel has survived and, despite its tiny size, it has become a force to be reckoned with in the world – technologically, militarily, and of course, spiritually. What typifies and defines Zionism is Israel's ability to return to its ancient homeland, accomplishing through hard work what Jews for two millennia could only dream of.

**The Official Return to Jewish Sovereignty:** David Ben-Gurion declares Israel's independence in Tel Aviv, beneath a large portrait of Theodor Herzl, founder of modern Zionism, on May 14, 1948 (5 Iyar 5708).

*"And may our eyes behold Your return to Zion, with mercy."*
(from the Amidah Prayer)

Jews around the world, wherever they were, would stand in prayer, thrice daily, facing east to the Land of Israel, and many of their prayers called for the rebuilding of what had been the sovereign kingdom of Israel for hundreds of years, in the era of King David, King Solomon, the prophets, and the judges. Nonetheless, for many, even most, the hope of returning home was out of the realm of realism. It was a surrealistic, intangible pipe dream that most Jews did not truly think would happen in their lifetimes. But then it started to happen. The hard-to-believe ancient prophecies that had referred to the return of Israel to its homeland began to come to fruition, incredibly, one by one.

*"But you, O mountains of Israel, shall yield your produce and bear your fruit for My people Israel, for their return is near."*
(Ezekiel 36:8)

This process of return to sovereignty in the ancient homeland has continued, but it has been more than just a physical rebirth. Indeed, it has led to a psychological reawakening for Israel. After being beaten down for so many years as a persecuted minority in other lands, always dependent on the goodwill of the not always gracious host nations, this tiny, but once confident nation gradually had its pride restored. These "new Jews" started to truly understand that they could stand on their own two feet and would no longer have to depend on the mercy of the rulers of the Gentile nations to survive and to thrive.

Having said all that, we have a concept in Judaism called "Hakarat HaTov," which refers to the obligation to show appreciation for the good that other people have done for us. While we are proud of our ability to pick ourselves up after centuries of adversity, it would be inaccurate to say that no righteous Gentiles have helped us along the way. There were certainly many courageous non-Jews who helped individual Jews to escape the Nazi Holocaust, and there were many allied soldiers who liberated the concentration camps and the death camps in Europe. Likewise, there have been several notable nations that have actively participated in the rebuilding process since 1948 and especially after the miraculous Six Day War in 1967, when the centrally located Biblical lands of Judea and Samaria (known to much of the world by the historically inaccurate term, the West Bank), as well as the reunited capital city, Jerusalem, fell back into Israel's hands, along with the strategic Golan Heights in the north, and other regions.

**A Biblical Nation in the Middle East:** From this map we can see a close-up of the Middle East, with little Israel [boxed] surrounded on three sides by the much larger Arab nations. The tiny regions of Judea and Samaria and Jerusalem are delineated in light brown in the heart of Israel.

Ever since 1948, the United States, far more than any other nation, has stood with and assisted the reestablished nation of Israel, both financially and politically. Under President Harry Truman, the United States was the first country to formally recognize Israel and to express its support. President Truman was known for his toughness, as exemplified by the famous campaign slogan, "Give

**God Put You in Your Mother's Womb:** President Harry Truman felt a deep emotional bond with Israel. He is presented here with a Chanukah candelabra as a special gift from Israeli Prime Minister David Ben-Gurion. Israeli Ambassador Abba Eban is looking on.

'em hell, Harry!" His visibly emotional moments were rare, but Israel was one topic that touched his heart.

Truman biographer David McCullough reported:

*"I have about three instances where Truman cried in public. They are very few and they are always real."* (4)

When Chief Rabbi Yitzchak Isaac HaLevi Herzog of the newly established state of Israel came to visit President Truman in early 1949, the two had a very moving exchange, in which the rabbi expressed his thanks to the president for his recognition of Israel. He then went on to say the following words to the president: "God put you in your mother's womb so that you could be the instrument to bring about the rebirth of Israel after almost two thousand years." Truman was visibly moved. Herzog then opened his Bible, and with the president reading along in his own Bible, the rabbi read from the Book of Ezra (1:2), in which the Persian King Cyrus spoke the following words:

*"The Lord, God of Heaven has given me all the kindness of the earth: and He has commanded me to build Him a house (Temple) at Jerusalem, which is in Judea."*

On hearing these words, Truman rose from his chair and with great emotion, tears glistening in his eyes, he turned to the Chief Rabbi and asked him if his actions for the sake of the Jewish people were indeed to be interpreted thus and that the hand of the Almighty was in the matter. The Chief Rabbi reassured him that he had been given the task once fulfilled by the mighty King of Persia, and that he too, like Cyrus, would occupy a place of honor in the annals of the Jewish people. [5]

In 1961, then Prime Minister of Israel David Ben-Gurion, on his final trip to the US, visited former President Truman in a New York hotel suite to express his appreciation once again:

*"I told him that as a foreigner, I could not judge what would be his place in American history; but his helpfulness to us, his constant sympathy with our aims in Israel, his courageous decision to recognize our new State so quickly and his steadfast support since then had given him an immortal place in Jewish history. As I said this, tears suddenly sprang to his eyes. And his eyes were still wet when he bade me goodbye. I had rarely seen anyone so moved. I tried to hold him for a few minutes until he had become more composed, for I recalled that the hotel corridors were full of waiting journalists and photographers. He left. A little while later, I too had to go out, and a correspondent came up to me to ask, 'Why was President Truman in tears when he left you?'"* [6]

While Truman's passionate and emotional love of Israel, which stemmed from his Christian faith that was rooted in the Hebrew Bible, was quite remarkable, there have been many other presidents, as well, who have been notable friends of the Jews as an ethnic or religious group, and have instinctively understood the importance of standing with Israel. These have included Presidents George Washington, John Adams, Thomas Jefferson, Abraham Lincoln, Theodore Roosevelt, Woodrow Wilson, Warren Harding, Herbert Hoover, Dwight Eisenhower, Lyndon Johnson, and John F. Kennedy, among others.

Even so, there have been American administrations that have been less supportive. President Jimmy Carter was a president who was known to blame Israel for the lack of peace in the Middle East. During his term in office, he tried to project public objectivity to enhance his mediator role, but in the decades that followed, Carter cultivated a warm relationship with the terrorist leadership of Hamas, insisting, against all historical fact, that the Israeli "occupation" of the West Bank "perpetrates even worse instances of apartness, or apartheid, than we witnessed even in South Africa." [7]

President Barack Obama had several noted head-to-head collisions with Israeli Prime Minister Benjamin Netanyahu, even forcing a temporary freeze on construction in Jewish communities in its Biblical heartland, Judea and Samaria. Often acting through surrogates, like Vice President Joe Biden, Secretary of State Hillary Clinton, and her successor, John Kerry, Obama's hostility to Israel was clear, and it often wasn't pretty, including several notable verbal skirmishes, both in the White House and on the phone. After one notable and particularly raucous in-person encounter with Obama and his team, the president stormed out, announcing that he was going to have dinner with his wife and daughter. Meanwhile, Netanyahu and his entourage were left alone in this White House meeting room to fend for their own dinner. [8]

The coup de grace came in the United Nations during Obama's last month in office. Working together with his Secretary of State John Kerry, Obama approved and actually orchestrated the American abstention in a UN Security Council resolution condemning "Israeli settlement building," thus letting it pass without an American veto, and thereby enabling it to be unanimously approved. According to transcripts released by the Egyptian daily *Al-Youm Al-Saba'a*, Secretary Kerry, along with National Security Adviser Susan Rice, had secretly met in advance with the Secretary General of the PLO Executive Committee Saeb Erekat and with Majed Faraj, head of the Palestinian Authority's General Intelligence Service, to plan cooperation in pushing through the resolution. [9]

After eight difficult years with Obama, the election of President Donald J. Trump was a unique breath of fresh air for friends of Israel. While much of the focus in the public, as well as the media, was on his out-of-the-box style and the fierce opposition to him from the Left, his consistently positive actions relating to Israel were often missed by many friends of Israel who already had him negatively typecast. The reality was that his actions were guided by the pragmatism that led to his success in the world of business in New York City. While his critics were turned off by his boisterousness and aggressive pursuit of his goals, when it came to Israel, he was very supportive in his statements, and, contrary to his predecessor, displayed humility and a willingness to learn about the difficult political challenges in the complicated Middle East. Whether he always came to the right conclusions, especially with his "Deal of the Century," can certainly be debated, but he will absolutely go down in history for some key accomplishments:

1. The moving of the US Embassy to Jerusalem and public recognition of Jerusalem as Israel's capital city.
2. The closing of the PLO shadow embassy in Washington, DC.

**Keeping the Promise:** On May 14, 2018, with many American and Israeli dignitaries present, a new plaque was unveiled dedicating the formal move of the US Embassy to Jerusalem. The out-of-the-box move by the Trump administration was ground-breaking. As opposed to the expected uptick in terrorism and war, it led to a surprising peace process between Israel and its Muslim neighbors.

3. The withdrawal from the dangerous Iran nuclear deal.
4. The (ignored) demand that the Palestinian Authority stop paying salaries to terrorists.
5. The official recognition of Israeli sovereignty over the strategic Golan Heights.
6. The official recognition that there is nothing "illegal" about Israeli communities in Judea and in Samaria.

All of these great accomplishments contributed to a strengthening of the ties between the United States

**Making America Tough Again:** President Donald Trump holds up a new presidential memorandum that reinstated nuclear sanctions on the Iranian regime. Trump reversed the appeasement policy towards Iran that had been dominant during the Obama-Biden years.

and Israel during Trump's tenure. The relationship developed to unprecedented heights, and while Israel benefited enormously, so did the United States. With Israel strategically placed at the junction of three major continents and with its unmatched intelligence and technological prowess, the envy of the world, the United States has cashed in on its support for Israel in countless ways that have rarely been reported in the media. The US has long relied on the Mossad and other Israeli intelligence agencies for information about terrorism, radical Islamic movements, weapons proliferation, and other Middle East-related events. The late Republican Senator Jesse Helms used to call Israel "America's aircraft carrier in the Middle East," when explaining why the United States viewed Israel as such a strategic ally, saying that the military foothold in the region offered by the Jewish state alone justified the military aid that the United States granted Israel every year. [10]

There have been many instances of cooperation in recent years. One such example was in 2017, when it was disclosed that Israeli cyber-operators penetrated a cell of bomb-makers in Syria. Israel passed on information indicating ISIS had learned to make explosives resembling laptop computer batteries, which can evade detection by airport X-ray machines and other screening devices. The information prompted the United States and the United Kingdom to ban large electronic devices in carry-on luggage on flights from ten airports in eight Muslim-majority countries to the US and the UK. [11]

For many years, there has been a broad bipartisan consensus among policy makers that Israel has advanced US interests in the Middle East and beyond. The leftward drift among Democrats has weakened that consensus in recent years, but most still would agree with the following statements of fact:

1. Israel has successfully prevented victories by radical nationalist movements in Lebanon and Jordan, as well as in Palestinian-controlled regions.
2. Israel has kept a watchful eye on Syria, providing intelligence as needed.
3. Israel's air force is predominant throughout the region.
4. Israel's frequent wars have provided battlefield testing for American arms, often against Russian-produced weapons.
5. Israel's intelligence service has assisted the US in intelligence gathering and covert operations.
6. Israel has missiles capable of reaching as far as the former Soviet Union, it possesses an extensive nuclear arsenal, and it has cooperated with the US military-industrial complex with research and development for new jet fighters and anti-missile defense systems. [12]

It should also be noted that due to the unprecedented intelligence-sharing, there was no Benghazi fiasco on Trump's watch. The Obama administration's pandering to the radicals in the Islamic world, combined with his intentional distancing from Israel, was reversed during the Trump years. Under Trump, Israel was publicly praised as a friend and ally. Since that closeness was not apologetic and was understood by all, the Arab nations became much more cooperative and willing to work together, not just with the United States, but also with

Israel, on multiple geo-political issues. The concern of the Arab Sunni nations from the very real threat from Shiite Muslim Iran was first and foremost in cultivating a relationship with the Jewish state, but covert trade and quiet cooperation on other issues soon became the norm rather than the exception, eventually leading to the full normalization of relations between Israel and Arab countries like the United Arab Emirates, Sudan, Bahrain, and Morocco.

Of course, Israel receives substantial military aid each year from the United States – 3.8 billion dollars per year to be exact. According to the Memorandum of Understanding between the two countries, 100% of that military aid to Israel must be spent on American arms, equipment, and services, which enables the United States to benefit economically, as well as strategically.

Many American detractors of Israel have charged that Israel receives the lion's share of US military aid. The very suggestion conjures the anti-Semitic demon of an all-powerful Israel lobby that has turned the US Congress into its pawn. But these figures, while reflecting official direct US military aid, are almost meaningless in comparison to the real costs and benefits of US military aid – above all, the lack of necessity for the enormous expense of American boots on the ground, which, unlike other US allies, like Germany, Japan, and South Korea, Israel has never requested. In reality, Israel receives only a very small fraction of American military aid, and all of that assistance is spent in the US to the benefit of the American economy.

US air and naval forces constantly need to patrol the Northern, Baltic, and China Seas to protect American allies in Europe and in the Pacific – all at American expense. Glimpses of the scale of these operations are afforded by incidents like the shadowing of a Russian ship in the Baltics, near run-ins between Chinese Coast Guard ships and US Navy ships dispatched to challenge Chinese claims in the South China Sea, and near collisions between US Air Force planes and their Chinese counterparts in the same area.

In striking contrast, no US plane has ever flown to protect Israel's airspace. No US Navy ship patrols to protect Israel's coast. And most importantly, no US military personnel are put at risk to ensure Israel's safety … Israel defends its own turf with its own troops. [13]

Clearly, Israel and the United States have a relationship that is built on common interests. An alliance is a relationship among people, groups, or states that have joined together for their mutual benefit or to achieve some common purpose, whether or not an explicit agreement has been worked out among them. In the case of these two countries, the agreement has been explicitly stated in writing, verbally shared, and unspoken, as well.

This bond goes way beyond the usual strategic commitments of allies. The connections are historical and yes, even Biblical. Lest people forget, Israel brought the Ten Commandments and the Bible to the world, but the United States eagerly adopted those guidelines for life and made them its raison d'etre, its moral basis at its very foundation.

*"I have examined all religions, as well as my narrow sphere, my straightened means, and my busy life would allow; and the result is that the Bible is the best Book in the world. It contains more philosophy than all the libraries I have seen."*

(John Adams, in a letter to Thomas Jefferson, December 25, 1813) [14]

*"That I am not a member of any Christian Church, is true; but I have never denied the truth of the Scriptures."*

(Abraham Lincoln, July 31, 1846) [15]

That philosophical foundation was firm among the Founders of the American nation, but even those that were not connected to any particular denomination, like Lincoln, considered the Bible to be the ethical/spiritual foundation on which the nation stood. Tragically, that foundation is under assault in today's America. Ideological forces that do not share its values are methodically working, on multiple levels across the nation, to dismantle the very pillars on which the United States was established. Yet, in order to understand the threat, one must first grasp the foundational structure of the values that are under assault. How have they impacted the nation? Most importantly, why are these values under attack when they are so critical for the survival of the United States of America?

*Chapter Two*
# Values of the American Republic

*"A Bible and a newspaper in every house, a good school in every district – all studied and appreciated as they merit – are the principal support of virtue, morality, and civil liberty."*

(Benjamin Franklin,
in a letter to the Ministry of France, March 1778) [1]

Ancient Israel received spiritual guidance through the conduit of the Biblical prophets, who spoke powerful words of divine rebuke when needed, and often when not desired. When Israel and its leadership veered in a counter-productive or morally corrupt direction, they could always count on words of conscience and direction, whether they requested it or not.

While not a prophet, Benjamin Franklin was a voice of morality and conscience in the American colonies. He spoke strongly against the unlimited rule of tyrants, but he also emphasized the need for leaders and citizens to follow the guidelines of Scripture as the way to constrain uncontrolled power.

In lieu of prophecy as a means of enforcing human integrity, this philosophy was eventually developed into the comprehensive system of governmental self-enforcement, which included the brilliant concepts of Separation of Powers and Checks and Balances, which helped prevent abuse and corruption. However, it is important to remember that the focus on balance between strong leadership and spiritual guidance came from Biblical lessons, as did the need for an enlightened, aware, and assertive citizenry.

The Bible, always known to the Jews as the Torah, was considered by the Founders of the United States to be the most basic and central element of education. This belief was so fundamental and was so widely accepted that it even permeated the halls of higher learning. A basic knowledge of Israel's ancient language, Hebrew, the original language of the Torah, was considered necessary for early American scholars: many universities made it a prerequisite in their core curriculum. In fact, Hebrew was compulsory at Harvard until 1787.

Harvard President, Increase Mather, who served as Harvard's chief administrator from 1685-1701, was an ardent Hebraist, as were his predecessors, Henry Dunster and Charles Chauncey. Mather's writings contain numerous quotations from the Talmud as well as from the works of Saadia Gaon, Rashi, Maimonides and other classic Jewish Bible commentators. To this day, Yale's insignia, which has been in use since 1736, has the Hebrew words *Urim V'Tumim*, meaning Light and Perfection, written on it. These words refer to the holy parchment on which God's Name is written. This parchment was positioned within the breastplate of the High Priest in the Temple in Biblical Jerusalem. Samuel Johnson, first president of King's College (1754-1763), the latter-day Columbia University, expressed the intellectual attitude of his age when he referred to Hebrew as "essential to a gentleman's education."

So prevalent and popular was the study of the Hebrew language in the Ivy League schools of the late 16th and early 17th centuries that several students at Yale

Dartmouth       Yale       Columbia

**God and Israel in the Ivy League:** There was a time when Israel and God were respected and even honored in the top American colleges. In these seals, the Hebrew language is displayed with references to God and Israel's Temple in Jerusalem. Will the thought police of the secular Left soon be demanding the removal of these words? (The Hebrew text is boxed in green to draw the reader's attention, but the boxes are not a part of the official seals.)

delivered their commencement addresses in Hebrew. Hebrew was one of three optional foreign languages in which a commencement speech could be given in the schools that taught the language. These schools included top universities such as Yale, Harvard, Columbia, Dartmouth, Brown, Princeton, Johns Hopkins, and the University of Pennsylvania. The two other languages allowed were Latin and Greek.

Beyond the educational sphere, the Jewish/Biblical influence could also be seen in the legal system. The 15 Capital Laws of New England included the "Seven Noahide Laws" of the Torah, or what may be termed the "seven universal laws of morality," the observance of which are incumbent upon all people. Six of these laws prohibit idolatry, blasphemy, murder, robbery, adultery, and eating flesh from a living animal, while the seventh requires the establishment of courts of justice. Such courts are essential for any society based on the need for reason and persuasion, rather than passion and intimidation. [2]

That very concept of human discourse is one that has often been forgotten in present-day America. In the midst of the Covid-19 crisis, the culture of left-wing terror erupted in all its force in the Spring of 2020, as the verbal violence, political correctness, woke culture, and litmus tests that were already on the rise, were supplemented by outright physical violence, including riots, looting, destruction of both public and private property, and calls to dismantle law enforcement by defunding the police. When it comes to any public affirmation of elements of the Judeo-Christian civilization on which the country was founded, the proverbial big brother described in George Orwell's "1984" is there to quickly reprimand and assault the messenger. In stark contrast to a philosophy of "let us reason together," anyone who dares to cross the red lines of the left-wing secular big brother is rapidly shot down with harsh intimidation, whether verbal or physical.

**Warned of Thought Control:** George Orwell's visionary writings expose the false idealism in socialism. The brilliance of his novels is that they reveal how tyranny, often masquerading as equality, breeds more tyranny, often even worse than that which it came to replace.

It was not always like this in the land of the free and the home of the brave. For instance, the American university was once the great bastion of intellectual discourse, where great ideas were discussed and debated, where questions of life and death, God and humanity were probed in depth, where the essential truths were analyzed, and where the meaning of truth and justice was explored and researched. Sadly, Orwell's Newspeak has taken over from the original vision of intellectual discourse that had been promoted by the Founding Fathers (heretofore, we will call them the Founders) of the American nation, a vision that was based on Judeo-Christian principles.

The Founders included such great visionaries (not an exhaustive list) as John Adams, Samuel Adams, Benjamin Franklin, Alexander Hamilton, Patrick Henry, Thomas Jefferson, James Madison, John Marshall, George Mason, and, of course, George Washington. They created the first modern nation-state based on genuine liberal principles. These included the marvelous concept that political sovereignty in any government resides in the citizenry – "We the people" – rather than in a divinely sanctioned monarchy; the capitalistic principle that economic productivity depends upon the release of individual energies in the marketplace rather than on state-sponsored policies; the moral principle that the individual, not the society or the state, is the sovereign unit in the political equation; and the judicial principle that all citizens are equal before the law. Moreover, this formula has become the preferred political recipe for success in the modern world, vanquishing the European monarchies in the 19th century and the totalitarian regimes of Germany, Japan, and the Soviet Union in the 20th century. [3]

# Leading Members Of
# The Founding Fathers Family

| | | |
|---|---|---|
| John Adams | Samuel Adams | Benjamin Franklin |
| Alexander Hamilton | Patrick Henry | Thomas Jefferson |
| James Madison | George Washington | John Marshall |

**A Merit-Based Leadership with a Firm System of Values:** The Founding Fathers were visionaries who established the concept of an American republic, a society based on inalienable rights and responsibilities.

More specifically, the Founders managed to defy conventional wisdom in four unprecedented achievements: first, they won a war for colonial independence against the most powerful military and economic power in the world; second, they established the first large-scale republic in the modern world; third, they invented political parties that institutionalized the concept of a legitimate opposition; and fourth, they established the principle of the legal separation of church and state, though it took several decades for that principle to be implemented in all the states. Finally, all these achievements were won without recourse to the guillotine or the firing squad, which is to say without the violent purges that accompanied subsequent revolutions in France, Russia, and China. [4]

Furthermore, it soon became clear that to become an American citizen would not be a matter of bloodlines or genealogy, but rather a matter of endorsing and embracing the values established at the founding of the nation. American society would be more open to talent than England or the rest of Europe, where hereditary bloodlines were essential credentials for entry into public life. The Founders comprised what Jefferson called "a natural aristocracy," meaning a political elite based on merit rather than genealogy, thus permitting brilliant men of impoverished origins such as Alexander Hamilton and Benjamin Franklin, who would have languished in obscurity in London, to reach the top tier of American leadership. [5]

All of the Founders agreed that American independence from Great Britain was nonnegotiable and that whatever government was established in lieu of British rule must be republican in character. [6] The concept of the

American republic, as opposed to democracy, is one that is often misunderstood. The emerging American nation was designed to be a republic, which included features of representative democracy, but went way beyond. In other words, it would be distinguishable from a pure democracy, or rule by the majority, for good or often for bad.

The American order is based on the idea that the United States consists of many different kinds of people in many different kinds of communities, and that each of these has interests that are legitimate even when they conflict with the equally legitimate interests of other communities. For example, the densely populous urban mode of life is not the only mode of life, and the people of the urban areas are not entitled by their greater numbers to dominate their fellow citizens in the less populous rural areas. [7]

The rights of minorities are further protected – from democracy – by the Constitution's limitations on the power of the federal government and specifically by the Bill of Rights, which places some considerations above democracy: freedom of speech, freedom of religion, freedom of the press, the right to keep and bear arms, the right to security in one's home and papers, etc. One of the main constitutional functions of the Supreme Court is to see to it that the federal government does not violate the Bill of Rights, even when "We the People" demand that it does. Rights that enjoy wide popular support require very little constitutional protection. It is the unpopular rights that require protection. [8]

The Electoral College ensures that the citizens in the less populous states are not reduced to serfdom by the greater numbers (and greater wealth) of the people in the more populous states. This balancing of minority rights with democratic processes is a fundamental part of the American order, and that principle is expressed through the Electoral College in the election of presidents. However, it should be pointed out that the value of pure democracy is purely procedural – majorities are at least as likely to be wicked and oppressive as virtuous and just. [9]

One is reminded of the "pro-democracy movement," otherwise known as the "Arab Spring," which erupted

**Not an Arab Spring:** The Arab world's pro-democracy movement proved once again what the elected Adolf Hitler proved eighty years ago. Unlimited democracy in the guise of "one person-one vote" can bring chaos, especially if those chosen by the people are intolerant and violently suppress the people's right to be free. Here we see Palestinians violently protesting the Abraham Accords, signed by Israel and several moderate Arab countries in 2020. Remember, Hamas was elected to majority rule in 2006 in the Palestinian Authority. Power to the people?

in the Middle East in 2011-2012. What much of the mainstream media was praising as a movement to bring freedom and human rights to the Islamic world, soon was exposed as an intolerant revolution, orchestrated by Muslim Brotherhood fundamentalists to dominate with their particular brand of intolerance. A 2010 poll was taken in several Islamic countries by the Pew Education Research Center in which it was found that while most people in countries like Egypt, Jordan, and Pakistan stated a preference for democracy, they also supported laws that most Americans would find abhorrent. For example, 77% of Egyptians were found to support cutting off the hands of an individual found guilty of theft, while a whopping 84% would support the death penalty for a Muslim who changes his or her religion. [10]

The Arab Spring represented a democratic revolution, absolute majority rule by the people, but certainly not an American-style republic, in which freedom of speech, freedom of the press, and freedom of religion are essential values that go hand-in-hand with an extraordinary tolerance towards those who have different opinions. In the emerging American system, there would be a higher vision, which would consider the role and values bequeathed to us by the Creator and His plans in the lives of the citizens.

*"And can the liberties of a nation be thought secure when we have removed their only firm basis, a conviction in the minds of the people that these liberties are the gift of God?"*

(Thomas Jefferson) [11]

The concept of the republic, as opposed to a democracy, was significant in that it set the tone of a higher law, which was critical in establishing the values of the nation. In a republic, as in many democracies, the people elect representatives to make the laws and an executive to enforce those laws. However, while, as in a democracy, the majority still rules in the selection of representatives, an official charter, in this case, the United States Constitution, lists and protects certain inalienable rights, thus protecting the minority from the arbitrary political whims of the majority. In this sense, republics like the United States function as "representative democracies," but essentially with a higher calling. [12]

In order to understand this concept, it is instructive to note that in the American concept of a constitutional republic, those inalienable rights are understood to come from God. They are not man-made and are not to be changed or removed. If they are, the government loses its God-given authority to rule. As it says in the Declaration of Independence:

*"We hold these truths to be self-evident, that all men are created equal, that they are endowed by their Creator with certain unalienable Rights, that among these are Life, Liberty and the pursuit of Happiness. – That to secure these rights, Governments are instituted among Men, deriving their just powers from the consent of the governed. – That whenever any Form of Government becomes destructive of these ends, it is the Right of the People to alter or to abolish it, and to institute new Government, laying its foundation on such principles and organizing its powers in such form..."* [13]

Unlike in a pure democracy, majority rule does not determine the direction. The Constitution, based on a higher law that comes from God, serves as the national compass. Because of that national compass, which serves as the conscience of the nation, even if a majority of the people descends into wickedness, the Constitution should, at least in theory, keep the nation on track.

That was the intention of those who founded the American republic, although there were a few notable exceptions that seemed to contradict the founding principles. For example, the practice of Slavery, which was widespread in colonial America, was incompatible with the values of the American Revolution, and all the prominent members of the Revolutionary generation acknowledged that fact. In three important areas they acted on this conviction: first, by ending the slave trade in 1808; second, by passing legislation in all the states north of the Potomac River, which put slavery on the road to ultimate extinction; and third, by prohibiting the expansion of slavery into the Northwest Territory. But

**The African Slave Trade:** Shackled Africans being taken into slavery by Muslim slave traders, approximately in the year 1700.

**Taken to America by Force:** African slaves being taken, against their will, on board a ship bound for the USA.

in all the states south of the Potomac, where some nine-tenths of the slave population resided, they failed to act.

Indeed, by insisting that slavery was a matter of state rather than federal jurisdiction, the Founding Fathers implicitly removed the divisive slavery question from the national agenda. This decision had catastrophic consequences, for it permitted the enslaved population to grow in size eightfold (from 500,000 in 1775 to 4,000,000 in 1860), mostly by natural reproduction, and to spread throughout all the southern states east of the Mississippi River. And at least in retrospect, the Founders' failure to act decisively before the slave population swelled so dramatically rendered the slavery question insoluble by any means short of civil war, which is what it ultimately led to.

There were at least three underlying reasons for this tragic failure. First, many of the Founders mistakenly believed that slavery would die a natural death, that decisive action was unnecessary because slavery would not be able to compete successfully with the wage labor of free individuals. They did not foresee the cotton gin and the subsequent expansion of the "Cotton Kingdom." Second, all the early efforts to place slavery on the national agenda prompted a threat of secession by the states of the Deep South (South Carolina and Georgia were the two states that actually threatened to secede, though Virginia might very well have chosen to join them if the matter came to a head), a threat especially potent during the fragile phase of the early American republic. While most of the Founders regarded slavery as a malignant cancer on the body politic, they also believed that any effort to remove it surgically would in all likelihood kill the young nation in the cradle. Finally, all conversations about abolishing slavery were haunted by the specter of a free African American population, most especially in those states that maintained slavery where in some locations, blacks outnumbered whites. None of the Founding Fathers found it possible to imagine a biracial American society, an idea that in point of fact did not achieve broad acceptance in the United States until the latter part of the 20th century.

Given these prevalent convictions and attitudes, slavery was that most un-American item, an inherently intractable and insoluble problem. As Jefferson so famously put it, the Founders held "the wolf by the ears" and could neither subdue him nor afford to let him go. Virtually all the Founders went to their graves realizing that slavery, no matter how intractable, would become the largest and most permanent stain on their legacy. And when Abraham Lincoln eventually made the decision

**Tikun Olam (Repairing the World):** On September 22, 1862, during the Civil War, the Great Emancipator, President Abraham Lincoln, issued a presidential proclamation and executive order, the Emancipation Proclamation, which decreed the end of American slavery.

that, at a terrible cost, ended slavery forever, he did so in the name of the Founders. [14]

The American experience has been personified by what we Jews call "Tikun Olam" or repairing and improving the world. In addition to the abolition of slavery and the granting of voting rights to women, American history has displayed what historian William Federer has described as a remarkable progression of religious tolerance:

*Originally, each colony had its own preferred Protestant denomination (Anglican, Puritan, Dutch Reformed, Lutheran, Presbyterian, Congregational, Baptist, Quaker, etc.). After the Revolutionary War, tolerance gradually extended to Catholics.*

*In the early 1800s, tolerance extended to liberal Christian denominations (such as Unitarians and Universalists). In the middle 1800s, persecuted Jews from Europe immigrated and were tolerated. In the late 1800s, anyone who believed in a monotheistic God was tolerated. In the early 1900s, tolerance began to extend to polytheists and many new religions. In the middle 1900s, tolerance extended to atheists. Finally, tolerance extended to radical anti-religious, radical homosexual groups, radical Muslim groups, etc., who teach intolerance toward the Judeo-Christian beliefs that began the entire progression of tolerance.* [15]

The Israeli experience has been quite different in many ways, but also similar in others. First of all, Israelis, more broadly known as the Jewish people, were slaves in ancient Egypt well over three thousand years ago. Just as Americans have learned that slavery is evil, due to their inability to end it sooner, Israelis know about slavery from the opposite perspective, that of being slaves themselves.

Emerging from slavery in Egypt, the former slaves received the Ten Commandments on Mount Sinai through their great leader, Moses, who subsequently wrote down and taught most of the Torah to the Israelites. Together with Israel's Oral tradition and countless related texts and commentaries, the Torah became the guidebook for our civilization and for the core of Western civilization.

Most of the teachings of Jesus, whose actual name was Yeshua, come from Judaism. Since he was a Jew who lived in the Land of Israel, that was quite natural. Many of his followers took things in a different direction, eventually evolving into a completely separate religion, rather than an offshoot of Judaism, but the roots of Christianity and many of its core values were learned from Judaism.

The American Founders understood this. Even some 130-160 years before the establishment of the modern State of Israel, American Presidents and Founders spoke and wrote about Israel, both Biblical and modern. The Founders, most of whom were Christians of deep faith, looked to Biblical history for inspiration and guidance. They frequently noticed striking parallels between Israel's miraculous story and the making of the American nation. Thomas Jefferson, who would eventually become the third president, served on a committee to draft a seal for the newly formed United States of America. This seal would characterize the spirit of the nation. He proposed the following representation: "The Children of Israel in the wilderness, led by a cloud by day, and a pillar of fire by night."

Distinguished philosopher/inventor/statesman Benjamin Franklin served on that same committee. Using the imagery of Moses lifting up his staff, and dividing the Red Sea, and Pharaoh in his chariot overwhelmed with the waters, he proposed this motto: "Rebellion to tyrants is obedience to God." [16]

Franklin's analogy was actually very appropriate and was similar in many ways to ancient Israel's vision of leadership. Despite the fact that monarchy or dictatorship was the international norm in Biblical times, Israel's form of monarchy was quite opposed to dictatorship or unrestricted political control. Samuel the Prophet, who was the moral conscience of Israel, followed divine guidance and appointed a king because the people demanded it, but he attached strings to the granting of their demand. First and foremost, the king would have to write his own Torah scroll and have it with him at all times, so that in making decisions for the people, he would always remember who is the real King and would act accordingly.

*"If you will fear the Lord and worship Him, and hearken to His voice and not rebel against the word of the Lord, then you and the king who reigns over you will be following the Lord your God. But if you do not hearken to the voice of the Lord, and you rebel against the word of the Lord, then the hand of the Lord will be against you, and against your fathers."*

(1 Samuel 12:13-15)

The Biblical commentator known as the Radak teaches that the words "your fathers" in the above quote refer to the kings of Israel. In other words, Samuel was giving a clear warning that the king was expected to adhere to God's Torah.

That was over three thousand years ago. The various forms of total or limited Jewish sovereignty in the Land of Israel lasted approximately one thousand years. The ideal that we have spoken about was not always achieved during that time period, but it was never forgotten as the ideal, and its significance did not escape the Founders of the United States of America, who founded their new nation on moral, Biblical principles.

After two thousand years of exile, the Jewish people have restored a form of sovereignty to the Land of Israel, which for most of that time was known to the world as Palestina, which was a Roman derivative of Philistines. In short, the Roman conquerors exiled the Jews, renaming their country after one of their many enemies.

For almost two thousand years the land laid dormant, but for the past 150 years, Jews have been gradually returning to and rebuilding their ancient land, while gradually restoring their sovereignty. In 1922, the League of Nations formally appointed Great Britain as the colonial power over what was then called Mandatory Palestine. [17] In the succeeding years, there were three Jewish national underground movements that rebelled against the British rule, eventually overthrowing the British Mandate, and declaring independence as the State of Israel in 1948, but the Arabs were not satisfied and continued their war against Israel, which had already begun in 1947.

In Israel's War of Independence, from 1947-1949, the surrounding Arab nations attacked Israel from all sides with forces and weaponry far beyond what Israel possessed, but Israel survived. At the end of the War of Independence, Israel had lost 1% of its population and was left with a truncated state, its land area smaller than the American state of New Jersey, with an almost

**Taken Captive by the Jordanian Army:** Jewish residents of the Jewish Quarter in the Old City of Jerusalem surrender to the Jordanians in 1948 during Israel's War of Independence.

defenseless belt just nine miles wide. [18]

This precarious situation remained until the 1967 Six Day War, when the Arab nations attempted to wipe out the tiny country, but in just six days, Israel recaptured its mountainous Biblical heartland of Judea and Samaria (the so-called West Bank), its ancient capital of eastern Jerusalem with the Temple Mount and the Western Wall, the strategic Golan Heights next to Syria in the North, and the regions of Gaza and Sinai, both of which Israel eventually returned to Arab control.

Israel today is a growing, very idealistic, and very young country. Paradoxically, despite its Biblical heritage, it was established in May of 1948 by mostly secular immigrants from eastern Europe, who were soon complemented by thousands of Holocaust survivors

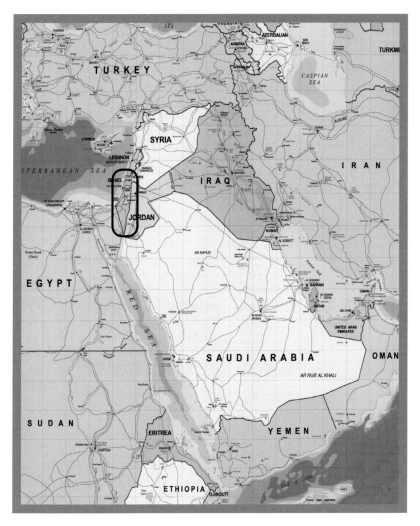

**A Jewish Speck in a Huge Arab Land Mass:** A view of the entire Middle East, gives one a sense of perspective, making crystal clear the absurdity of demanding Israeli surrender of land.

| Country | Land Mass In Square Miles | Number Of Times Israel Could Fit Into This Country |
| --- | --- | --- |
| Israel | 8,367 | |
| Lebanon | 4,015 | 0 |
| Jordan | 35,637 | 4 |
| Syria | 71,498 | 9 |
| Iraq | 168,754 | 20 |
| Turkey | 301,383 | 36 |
| Egypt | 384,343 | 46 |
| Iran | 636,296 | 76 |
| Saudi Arabia | 756,985 | 90 |

**A Genuine Sense of Perspective:** Even though it is a tiny country, about the size of New Jersey, Israel is always asked to surrender historic strategic parts of its homeland for the promise of peace. Looking at this comparison, one can see how that would be suicidal for Israel.

from all over Europe, as well as several hundred thousand mostly religious refugees, who were expelled from the surrounding Arab countries. While its status as a vibrant parliamentary democracy is enshrined in its Declaration of Independence, so is its status as a Jewish state. The tension between those two elements is ever-present, as the segments of the population that want to strengthen the Jewish religious values in the country

**From Slavery to Freedom:** Jews celebrate Passover by worshipping at the Western Wall in the Old City of Jerusalem on Passover 2019. Thousands of Jews make the pilgrimage to Jerusalem during the eight-day Passover holiday, which commemorates the Israelites' exodus from slavery in Egypt some 3,500 years ago.

have increased in numbers in recent decades, and that trend is continuing. [19]

As opposed to the United States, which studies have shown, has gradually become more secular and less conservative in its values on issues such as the traditional family, abortion, school prayer, school choice, and religious liberty, Israel has gradually moved closer to religion and to conservatism on all of those issues, including national pride and assertiveness. [20]

These trends actually bring Israel's current value structure closer in sync with the half of America whose values have been under attack – those who cherish traditional American values and hope to reverse the secularization trends, the Marxist assault, the race-baiting, and the bitter identity politics that aims to intimidate those who don't follow the hard Left party line. These Americans have been pained to see the wild destruction of classic American monuments, the rampant looting in the heart of American cities, the violent attacks on law enforcement, as well as the systematic assault on traditional values in America's public schools, colleges and universities.

The terrible culture war in the United States, as well as other parts of the free world, will continue to be fought. One would have hoped that it would happen as a spirited discourse in the free market of ideas, although it seems highly unlikely. There are significant forces in America that would prefer to "shut down" all of those who disagree with them, in order to further their revolutionary goals, even if those goals are in conflict with American values as enshrined in the Bill of Rights. The intensity of this culture war has been increasingly leading to confrontation, and those forces of intolerance seem to be on the rise.

## Chapter Three

# Domestic Terrorism is Not Social Justice

*"If you want to be wrong, then follow the masses."*

(Socrates) [1]

*"What has violence ever accomplished? What has it ever created? No martyr's cause has ever been stilled by an assassin's bullet. No wrongs have ever been righted by riots and civil disorders. A sniper is only a coward, not a hero; and an uncontrolled or uncontrollable mob is only the voice of madness, not the voice of the people."*

(Robert F. Kennedy) [2]

Minneapolis: May 25, 2020 – George Floyd Jr. was a black American man killed during an arrest after allegedly passing a counterfeit $20 bill in Minneapolis. He previously had been convicted of eight crimes, including armed robbery, but that was not his claim to fame in this instance. What made George Floyd famous, even a folk hero of sorts, was that he was killed by a white police officer who, while trying unsuccessfully to force him into the police car, knelt on Floyd's neck for nearly eight minutes, eventually killing him. This act of brutality received nearly universal condemnation across the political spectrum and sparked some of the most massive internal street violence and social strife that the United States has ever experienced. [3]

There have been other incidents in which a white cop killed a black civilian under questionable circumstances, usually while the cop was trying to make an arrest.

The Floyd incident, as bad as it was, was not the first of its kind leading to massive street protests, although it certainly has gotten the most attention. Some of the others in recent years have included the following:

### *July 17, 2014: Eric Garner*

Eric Garner died after he was wrestled to the ground while resisting arrest by a New York police officer on suspicion of illegally selling cigarettes.

Reportedly in a choke hold, the 395-pound Garner, who had previously been arrested by the NYPD thirty times, uttered the words "I can't breathe" eleven times. The incident – filmed by a bystander – led to protests across the country. The police officer involved was later fired but not prosecuted. It came a year after the Black Lives Matter movement emerged in response to the acquittal of the man who killed teenager Trayvon Martin in Florida.

### *August 9, 2014: Michael Brown*

Michael Brown, 18, was killed by a police officer in Ferguson, Missouri, who was responding to reports that Brown – who was not armed – had stolen a box of cigars. The exact circumstances of the encounter are disputed, but Brown was shot six times, according to autopsy reports. According to the Justice Department report, when the officer tried to stop Brown and his friend, Brown reached through the driver's side window of the officer's vehicle and began punching him. The department noted that some witnesses claimed Brown never put his hands in the car – but said those testimonies did not corroborate physical and forensic evidence. The officer involved resigned from the force but was not prosecuted. The incident led to multiple waves of protests and civil unrest in Ferguson, boosting the Black Lives Matter movement further. [4] [5]

## *November 22, 2014: Tamir Rice*

Tamir Rice, a boy of 12, was shot dead in Cleveland, Ohio by a police officer. Police had been called to the scene after someone reported that a "guy" was pointing a gun at people, adding that the weapon could be a "fake" and the man in question could actually be a juvenile – the additional information was not passed along to the officers. Police claimed that they told Rice to drop the weapon – but instead of dropping it, he pointed it at them. In this tragic incident, the police were only able to confirm that the gun was a toy after Rice had been shot dead. The Cleveland officers involved in the Tamir case were ultimately not charged after the Justice Department said the video footage of the incident was of too poor quality to conclusively provide evidence to bring a federal criminal civil rights prosecution. [6]

## *April 4, 2015: Walter Scott*

Walter Scott was shot in the back five times by a white police officer, who was later fired and eventually sentenced to 20 years in prison. Mr. Scott had been pulled over for having a defective light on his car in North Charleston, South Carolina, and ran away from the police officer after a brief scuffle. The killing sparked protests in North Charleston, with chants of "No justice, no peace."

### *July 5, 2016: Alton Sterling*

Alton Sterling's death led to days of protests in Baton Rouge, Louisiana. Mr. Sterling was killed after police responded to reports of a disturbance outside a shop. The two officers involved did not face criminal charges, but one was dismissed and the other suspended from the police.

### *July 6, 2016: Philando Castile*

Philando Castile was pulled over by the police during a routine check. He told them he was licensed to carry a weapon and had one in his possession. He was shot as he was reaching for his license, according to his girlfriend, who was standing nearby, but the officer said that Castile was reaching for his gun. The officer involved was cleared of murder charges.

### *March 18, 2018: Stephon Clark*

Stephon Clark died after running away from police and being shot at least seven times by Sacramento, California police, who were investigating a break-in.

The district attorney said that the police had not committed a crime, as the officers said they feared for their lives, believing Mr. Clark was armed, even though only a mobile phone was found at the scene. The release of a police video of the incident sparked major protests in the city.

### *March 13, 2020: Breonna Taylor*

Breonna Taylor, a 26-year-old former emergency medical technician, was shot eight times when officers raided her apartment in Louisville, Kentucky. The police were executing a search warrant as part of a narcotics raid, based on her relationship with her drug-running ex-boyfriend, but in this raid, no drugs were found. Nonetheless, her current boyfriend, Kenneth Walker, who was present, fired first, causing the police to return fire after the officer was shot and wounded. One policeman involved was fired and the two others were put on administrative leave after the shooting. One of them was eventually convicted of reckless endangerment, due to the amount and direction of the shots that apparently were fired in self-defense, but that damaged a neighboring apartment. [7]

Proportionately, these incidents have been few and far between when compared to the thousands of arrests that end successfully. Furthermore, the killings of unarmed black Americans by white cops have been tiny in number, when compared to the thousands of black Americans who are killed in American cities by other black Americans every year. According to former New York City Mayor Rudolph Giuliani:

*"The unarmed shootings – which are the ones that are the troublesome ones – there are only nine of them against blacks – twenty against whites in 2019. So that'll give you a sense. Meanwhile, there were 9,000 murders of blacks, 7,500 of which were black-on-black."*[8]

However, none of those killings have ever led to mass protests against the African Americans who have committed those crimes. Do black lives only matter when a white person does the killing?

The pattern has become clear. If a white cop kills a black suspect, there will be accusations of racism, there will be protests, and they will sometimes be substantial, depending on the particular incident, as well as current political factors.

All of the white cop – black victim incidents made headlines and led to protests against police brutality, some of them violent, but none of those protests reached the levels of the wild demonstrations that were sparked by the killing of George Floyd. Was the killing of Floyd somehow more heinous than the others? Not necessarily. According the autopsy report, the cause of death was "cardiopulmonary arrest complicating law enforcement subdual, restraint, and neck compression." That conclusion, death due to heart failure, showed that the case wasn't so cut-and-dry. [9] Furthermore, he was on drugs at the time of his arrest, he was seen resisting arrest, as were some of the others that were described above before being brutally killed. And even though he was turned into a folk hero after the shooting, he was certainly not a great model of noble behavior. His past record of convictions vouches for that.

The main difference was the timing. 2020 was an election year, and Trump's booming economy had already been hit hard by the Covid pandemic, so the Floyd killing was an opportunity for the Left to galvanize its forces. CNN, MSNBC, and the other talking heads for the Dems were on board, as were the corporate funders, all of whom were only too happy to breathe new life into the "systemic racism" narrative.

It should be noted that some of the previous incidents occurred during the presidency of Barack Obama, the first African American president. After some of the cases cited above, even in the earlier Trayvon Martin case, in which the accused (not a police officer) was eventually acquitted in a court of law, Obama quickly identified publicly with the presumed black victim, rather than trusting the legal system to do its job. Furthermore, he was praised by the left-wing media for doing so, rather than being questioned about his own biases in ignoring the presumption of innocence.

With Trump, it was sharply different. Despite his many accomplishments that benefitted African Americans, including job expansion, prison reform, and expanding economic opportunity zones, Trump became one of the main targets of the protests, and, perhaps spurred on even further by the fact that it was an election year, the Democrats and their media allies cynically poured lighter fluid on the fuming coals of the anti-Trump bandwagon, exploiting the situation to mercilessly attack the president. Given the many months of massive "Floyd protests" that followed, and the accompanying political self-righteousness and harsh accusations coming from the Left and directed at Trump, one could have been forgiven for thinking that the president himself masterminded the Floyd killing.

In any case, the descent into violent armed conflict did not occur right away. After Floyd's death, mass demonstrations protesting police violence against black people quickly erupted in cities throughout the United States, and even a few countries overseas. Many of these protests were peaceful at first, but what soon evolved into a mass protest movement in America's largest cities, was reported in much of the left-wing media, including the New York Times, as being spontaneous. [10]

It was soon proven to be anything but that, as protests quickly transformed into riots, and eventually into a form of low-level armed insurrection of a kind that we in Israel have experienced for many years. In America, it was something relatively new, and very disturbing, but one thing that we Israelis have learned is that any protest movement that involves violence and weapons of any kind cannot be spontaneous. There is always a radical, violent terrorist organization, or organizations, masterminding the strategic descent into violence from behind the scenes. Very often, they are well-funded by other less overtly violent left-wing organizations and/ or individuals that provide funding and logistics to accomplish their political goals through the violence.

In the first few days of the Floyd protests, much of the physical violence was sporadic, but there was quite a lot of verbal violence and intolerance expressed by the left-wing protesters towards the police, towards their political opponents, and even towards some liberal allies and apologists such as Minneapolis Mayor Jacob Frey. The case of the bleeding-heart liberal Frey was particularly revealing. The Democrat mayor, apparently holding back tears at a press conference shortly after the attack, commented that the protests stemmed from built-up anger and sadness "ingrained in our black community not just because of five minutes of horror, but 400 years." He added: "If you're feeling that sadness and that anger, it's not only understandable, it's right." [11]

Unfortunately for Frey, those soothing words of empathy did not satisfy the crowd of demonstrators that had already been hypnotized by the mushrooming mob psychology that was becoming increasingly violent and was beginning to sense its ability to exploit the white liberal guilt over the American past of slavery and lack of racial equality, in order to achieve their anarchist goals. Like a boxer who notices blood on his opponent's swollen face and recognizing weakness, starts peppering his face with repeated jabs to the wound, the emboldened mobs of the Left started to make demands to defund the police, which essentially meant to dismantle police departments across America, thereby handing over control of what were already crime-ridden streets in many American cities to the criminals.

It seemed as if no one could resist jumping on the anti-police bandwagon, especially the politicians. When the Democrats' 2020 presidential candidate, former Vice-President Joe Biden, was asked about the demands from many in his party to "defund the police" in the wake of the protests across the country, he responded that some funding should "absolutely" be "redirected" from the police. [12]

It was an interesting semantic sleight of hand that did not fool too many people, not even in Biden's own party, although that was the obvious goal, to soften the wording to seem more moderate to the suburban independents whose votes he desired (and eventually received in large numbers), but to wink to the growing AOC wing of the party. Anarchy was indeed the goal of the demand to dismantle police departments, but anyone who dared to point that out publicly or who dared to state that "all lives matter," including the lives of black police officers who were under attack from the rioters, was called a racist and was pressured to apologize, and many did, including senators, mayors, college presidents, teachers, social media stars, Hollywood stars, and rappers.

This was verbal terrorism of the worst kind, and that is certainly not to minimize the horror of actual physical terror attacks. We in Israel know that horror first-hand, myself included. As one who was shot and wounded by Palestinian terrorists along with my then three-year-old son who was shot in the head, and as one who knows and has known many hundreds of terror victims in Israel, I can confirm that the purpose of terrorism, aside from killing and wounding innocent civilians, is to aggressively intimidate and frighten people. That is the more subtle goal, which is strategically no less important to the terrorists' leadership that essentially wants to use that fear to attain its revolutionary political goals. The intent is that people will be afraid to say things that the radicals consider "politically incorrect," even if factually correct. That is the connection between physical terrorism and verbal terrorism.

Almost two weeks after Floyd's death, as the protests in Minneapolis and elsewhere continued to spread and intensify, a particularly vociferous group of protestors led by the advocacy group Black Visions demonstrated outside Mayor Frey's home, shouting their demands, among them the complete dismantling of the Minneapolis police department. In the noble spirit of brotherly love that most well-meaning liberals claim to believe in, and perhaps in the spirit of liberal shame for his so-called white privilege, the mayor emerged from his home to show his identification with the protestors.

The black-masked Frey was covered up to protect himself from the large crowd that was closely gathered together despite the Covid-19 pandemic, but at least one observer watching the intimidated, masked mayor standing at attention, commented that he looked like a frightened, emasculated prisoner of war. Frey meekly told the protest organizers that he had been "coming to grips with my own responsibility, my own failure in this" and said there needed to be "deep-seated, structural reform" within the Minneapolis Police Department.

**Guilty as Charged by the Tribunal:** Minneapolis Mayor Jacob Frey, torn between his liberal guilt and common sense, is confronted publicly by a member of the Black Visions Collective during a mass demonstration calling for the Minneapolis Police Department to be fully defunded. Frey, at first, tried to avoid the direct yes or no question about whether he would support defunding. After he was forced to answer with an honest "No," the vulgar-mouthed questioner, cheered on by the riled up crowd, ordered him to go home.

Then, as the mob of hundreds were listening, one of the leading protest organizers asked him whether he would commit at that moment to defunding the police department, and she demanded that the mayor answer the question with a simple "yes" or "no."

After some hesitation, Frey softly responded, by shaking his head and saying, "I do not support the full abolition of the police department." In response, the organizer grabbed the microphone from him and

**Go Home Jacob, Go Home**: Mayor Jacob Frey was reprimanded harshly by the agitated mob as he obediently followed the demand that he immediately leave the rally for not agreeing to abolish the police department. Had he not made the quick exit, it's very possible that he would have been violently attacked by the enraged crowd of demonstrators.

shouted at him to "get the f--k out of here."

As he slowly and carefully walked away, passing through the now riled up crowd almost as if heading to a firing squad, the protesters pointed accusing fingers at him, chanting in unison, "Go home, Jacob. Go home!" [13]

That was perhaps the turning point that exposed the true intentions of what the mainstream media had been calling a "peaceful protest" movement, for what it really was – a low level revolution – a combination of verbal abuse, riots, looting, and destruction – with the intention of applying pressure through a combination of physical and verbal violence to achieve political demands.

Rep. Ilhan Omar (D-MN) went beyond calls to defund the police, instead calling for the complete dismantling of the Minneapolis Police Department because it is "rotten to the root. We need to completely dismantle the Minneapolis Police Department. Because here's the thing, there's a cancer," she said, "The Minneapolis Police Department is rotten to the root, and so when we dismantle it, we get rid of that cancer." [14] These demands were the manifestation of an all-out violent assault on American values, with the goal of destroying Judeo-Christian civilization at its core.

The following months proved that there was nothing spontaneous about all of this turmoil. There was nothing spontaneous about the piles of bricks that were conveniently stationed on the street corners of Manhattan, nothing spontaneous about the mass looting of stores in New York City, Minneapolis, Los Angeles, and many other large American cities, and there was certainly nothing spontaneous about the murders and the other attacks on innocent people who were trying to protect their businesses or those of others. Furthermore, the rioting and the violent attacks on police officers of all colors were a blatant expression of disdain for law and order, while the rampant looting represented an assault on the American system of capitalism that enables any American to attain wealth through the sweat of his brow, a sacred American value which so many of these stores represented. In most cases, the relative wealth of its owners had been acquired through many years of hard work, but the rioters and the looters had no respect for that. Their recurring charge was "systemic racism," which admittedly did exist in pre-abolition America and in pre-Civil Rights Act America, but such a charge is no

**Shutting Down Macy's, Shutting Down Manhattan:** The Macy's flagship store is seen boarded up after a night of violent protests and looting in Midtown Manhattan on June 2, 2020 in New York City. In spite of a police-enforced 11 pm curfew, dozens of stores, including many high-end establishments, were ransacked during the previous evening's violent clashes between the NYPD and "protesters."

longer valid. The longer-term goal of the anarchists, or at least their leadership, was to destroy the American free market, a system in which anyone can advance and work his way up the ladder of success. The rioters wanted none of that. Their strategy seemed to be for the moment, to create chaos, to foment turmoil, and eventually, to claim the spoils of their multi-level revolution.

In cities like Seattle, in the state of Washington, where the CHAZ, or the Capitol Hill Autonomous Zone (later renamed the slightly less threatening CHOP, or Capitol Hill Organized Protest) was established, and where a major police precinct was abandoned by the police and vandalized by the radical activists, liberal politicians permitted anarchism to wreak havoc as both people

**Violence, Vandalism, and Shutdowns for the Radical Revolution:** An image of radical 1960's activist Angela Davis is displayed above the entrance to the vacated Seattle Police Department's East Precinct in the Capitol Hill Autonomous Zone (CHAZ) in Seattle, where lawless radicals took over a neighborhood. For weeks, they looted stores, refusing entry to law enforcement and small business owners, all the while claiming that they were protesting "systemic racism."

and property were assaulted in the streets. Rather than backing her Seattle Police Department (SPD), Democrat Mayor Jenny Durkan defended the radicals who had occupied and created turmoil in this neighborhood and she banned law enforcement from entering the zone, additionally issuing a ban on the use of tear gas by police, even outside the zone. [15]

The stark political divide became crystal clear in this city as Democrat city, county, and state representatives joined demonstrators on the front lines in the first week of June, when the increasingly embattled police

**People's (Communist) Republic of CHAZ:** A barricade set up at an entrance to the "Capitol Hill Autonomous Zone" in Seattle. The prominently displayed numbers/abbreviation, "1312 ACAB", are the number and letter equivalent of "All Cops Are Bastards". The message is clear and the goals (Anarchy, Revolution, etc) implied in the message are even clearer.

force used flash bangs and pepper spray on the mobs of increasingly emboldened demonstrators. [16]

The moral support from the leftist politicians helped to encourage the violence of the anarchists, as just one day later, the SPD reported that the crowd was throwing rocks, bottles, fireworks, and shining green lasers into officers' eyes.

Meanwhile, the delusional Mayor Durkan, who possibly was suffering remorse at having missed the opportunity to put flowers in her hair at the 1968 Woodstock Music Festival, gushed exuberantly at what she called the "Summer of Love" that would soon be taking place in her city. Furthermore, as she ordered the police to stay away from the zone, she stood by unmoved during the rampant internal violence there, as multiple civilians, including teenagers, were killed and wounded (not by the police), as businesses in the zone were plundered, and as left-wing radicals of various races set up barricades, all the while claiming that this was all about fighting against "white supremacy and racism." [17]

The catchy, but deceptive slogan "black lives matter," derived from the radical Marxist (and, by the way, anti-Semitic) political organization of the same name, became the mantra of this armed insurrection in some of America's largest cities, as most Democrats, a few gullible Republicans such as the pathetic Mitt Romney, and even a few ignorant foreign politicians leapt on the BLM bandwagon, eagerly parroting the slogan to any willing microphone.

The growing self-confidence of the broader black resistance movement has been reflected in the renewed demands for reparations for the past slavery of blacks in America. Those demands had already been presented in 2017 by a coalition of activist organizations in the Black Lives Matter movement, who released a policy platform that included a call for reparations for slavery. The Movement for Black Lives said in a statement that it aimed to stop the "increasingly visible violence against black communities." More than 50 organizations helped develop the platform, including Black Alliance for Just Immigration, the Black Youth Project 100, and the Black Leadership Organizing Collaborative. [18]

The fact that white people living in America today had nothing to do with past slavery did not matter to the "useful idiots" in the Democratic party, many of whom went along with the radical narrative, blaming all white Americans, and demanding reparations from all American taxpayers, for the slavery that neither they nor most of their ancestors had anything to do with. [19]

How easily we forget that most Americans who happen to be white, or Asian, or Hispanic, are immigrants or descendants of hard-working legal immigrants who came to America from other countries. Why in the world should they have to pay reparations to black Americans? Furthermore, a large percentage of black Americans are themselves immigrants, or children of immigrants, and therefore, are not descendants of American slaves. Last but not least, the fact is, that even before abolition, only a small minority of Americans were slave owners. To accuse all white Americans of being guilty of slavery, or even of being descended from slave owners, is a slanderous, outrageous claim, since only a tiny percentage can actually trace their roots to slave owners.

Therefore, when we put all of those facts together, the demand for reparations is in and of itself, patently racist in that it demands monetary reparations based solely on skin color, not on historical fact. [20]

Does past slavery and discrimination against African Americans justify the current reverse racism against all Americans? That is the question that far too many well-intentioned Americans are afraid to ask.

*Chapter Four*

# Escalating Demands Amid Low-Level Warfare

*"If you have always believed that everyone should play by the same rules and be judged by the same standards, that would have gotten you labeled a radical 60 years ago, a liberal 30 years ago and a racist today."*

(Thomas Sowell, American economist) [1]

*"Terrorism is the tactic of demanding the impossible and demanding it at gunpoint."*

(Christopher Hitchens, American author) [2]

The unjustified demands have multiplied as the BLM and Antifa goon squads have sensed weakness. With the implicit threat of violence, they have also targeted the business community, many of whom are themselves minorities, and often immigrants, who have struggled through years of hard work to get ahead.

With brazen demands that have made it clear that the lives of other minorities do not matter, many small businesses were ordered by BLM activists to have 23% black workers and to buy 23% of their supplies from black-owned businesses. In some cases, businesses that did not accept these demands were ominously threatened with closure by the BLM activists. Fernando Martinez, a Cuban immigrant, and partner of a restaurant group in Louisville, Kentucky was forced to close his restaurant due to pressure from the protesting mobs. The protesters were demanding that all local businesses in his neighborhood increase the representation of black products in their stores and black people in their staffs, among other demands. Martinez, who denounced the demands, said he was threatened by the protesters. [3]

Martinez later explained that his issue was not with Louisville's black community but with "socialism," which he said he escaped in leaving Cuba for the US. "We're here to work. We are dreamers. We're people who love freedom and love this country," Martinez said about Cuban-Americans. "This is not a race fight. This is an idea fight." [4]

It did not matter to the BLM hypocrites that the great Dr. Martin Luther King Jr. had dreamed of, and eloquently expressed, the goal of an America in which

**No to Racism, No to Violence, No to Riots, No to Looting:** Martin Luther King Jr. was a peaceful crusader for justice, but not for violence and not for lawlessness. He is seen speaking here at the 1963 March on Washington, during which he delivered his historic "I Have a Dream" speech, calling for all people to be judged "by the content of their character."

**Victim of Mob Violence:** Retired Police Captain David Dorn was murdered by rioters and looters who objected to his noble defense of law and order. This horrible murder of a caring man trying to do good was virtually ignored in the mainstream media. Perhaps if he had been murdered by a white cop it would have gotten some attention?

people would be judged by the content of their character, not by the color of their skin.

One shocking example of this hypocrisy, witnessed during this crisis in American cities and in the biased mainstream media, occurred in St. Louis, Missouri in the early hours of June 2, 2020. The incident occurred during the George Floyd protests in the Missouri city where they were ostensibly protesting against racism. A mob of black men, some of whom had previously been convicted of violent crimes, was looting a pawn shop in St. Louis, which was owned by a friend of David Dorn, a 77-year-old African American retired police captain. When the mob broke in, and the store alarm sounded, Dorn rushed to the shop to help his friend. Rather than fleeing the scene, the mob attacked Dorn, and he was fatally shot.

Somehow, the killing of Dorn was given minimal coverage in the mainstream media, which failed to grasp the tragic irony, that a retired black cop would be murdered by black looters for defending law and order, as a result of a "demonstration" ostensibly protesting police racism. No one seemed to notice the blatant racism in the fact that Dorn's murder would have merited far more media attention and popular protest if he had been killed by a white man. Adding to the irony, Dorn was murdered outside his friend's pawn shop, which was located on Martin Luther King Drive, but the cheering rioters, along with the adoring media did not seem to notice nor did they seem to care about that irony either. [5] [6]

*"Nonviolence is absolute commitment to the way of love … Violence as a way of achieving racial justice is both impractical and immoral."*

(Martin Luther King Jr.) [7]

In New York City, Manhattan was completely shut down by several days of rampant looting that totally ravaged all of the upscale shops and department stores, turning the "city that never sleeps" into a ghost town in which the politicians tied the hands of the police, so the looters literally controlled the streets.

The anarchists were allowed to take over the Big Apple, which empowered them to make their demands, and the left-wing politicians complied.

NYC Mayor Bill DeBlasio praised the slashing of a

full one billion dollars from the six billion NYPD budget [8] and then spent the rest of 2020 watching the attacks on police officers (of all colors) skyrocket as the murder and other violent crime rates on civilians soared. The goal was to keep the "protestors" happy by weakening the police, but the no-brainer result was to encourage every criminal suspect to attack the police and resist arrest. According to the radicals, if the arresting officer was forced to shoot the suspect to defend himself and to do his job, and if the cop was black, then he deserved the stress for serving the capitalist, racist regime. If he was white, then the demonstrators would have an excuse to heat up the rioting, looting, and attacking of public institutions, as well as innocent individuals.

Never mind stopping violent crime against innocent people of all colors. After the police were defunded in NYC, the already weakened police force was clearly on the defensive and struggled just to survive. Street crime in NYC skyrocketed in August 2020, with a 166% rise in shootings and a 47% rise in murders. [9] Even the NYPD chief of police was physically attacked by BLM agitators, while he and his colleagues were trying to protect a peaceful prayer march by faith leaders. [10]

While all of this madness was taking place, the Democrats were sitting back and watching quietly as the cities burned, with some even cheering it on. It soon became apparent that established national politicians on the Left were, in effect, supporting the violent riots and looting, not just with their silence, but often, with some very public statements, as in the case of then candidate for president, Senator Kamala Harris (D-CA). Harris made it clear whose side she was on with a June 1 tweet, "If you're able to, chip in now to the @

**Vulgarity & Vandalism & Defunding:** Making a mockery of the words "peaceful protest", leftist demonstrators affiliated with Black Lives Matter (BLM) and other groups defaced the statue, "New York in Its Infancy", outside the New York Surrogate Court building near City Hall. The artist's work was a representation of British, Dutch, and Indian influence in early NYC. Tensions had been on the rise ahead of a City Council vote on New York's budget, which resulted in the defunding of the NYPD. Since the defunding, street crime has skyrocketed in the Big Apple.

MNFreedomFund to help post bail for those protesting on the ground in Minnesota." [11]

If they were really protesting peacefully, which we now know that many weren't, why would they need bail so badly? Despite, or maybe because of, Harris's strong identification with the radicals, she was chosen as her party's candidate for vice president. Her running-mate, Joe Biden, who had become the Democrats' nominee for president, laughed off the brutal violence of Antifa during a televised debate with his opponent, President Donald Trump. Asked by Trump to condemn

**Sad Descent into Third-Worldism:** A beaten and bloodied Trump supporter was assaulted by Antifa thugs in Black Lives Matter Plaza in Washington, DC on November 14, 2020. He was kicked and stomped on while on the ground, and once the lynch mob cleared out, his friends assisted him. The peaceful pro-Trump rally had attracted tens of thousands who came to protest electoral fraud in the November 3rd presidential election. After nightfall, when the crowds had significantly thinned out, the Antifa terrorists appeared and mob-attacked individual Trump supporters.

Antifa's violence, Biden would only say that the radical organization was just "an idea."

Sure, just ask the bloodied and wounded pro-Trump supporters who were attacked in DC's Black Lives Matter Plaza by Antifa thugs on November 10, 2020, just one week after Election Day. Ask the peaceful Trump supporters who were brutally assaulted, whether Antifa is just an idea, as Biden and Harris disingenuously wanted the voters to believe. And then there was Portland, a beautiful city of tall lovely trees and surrounding greenery, which also happens to be a notorious bastion of the radical Left. For more than three months, Black Lives Matter and Antifa demonstrators, many wearing black helmets and hoods (KKK resemblance anyone?), clashed daily with police and with federal agents who had been sent to stop the attempts to vandalize and overrun federal property in the city. They also marched through and destroyed private property in predominantly black neighborhoods, prompting negative reaction from members of the black community. One prominent black leader wrote to Mayor Ted Wheeler, pointing out that the demonstrators were 99% white and complaining that some clashes had unfolded three blocks from his house. "It has nothing to do with helping black people. These hoodlums are needlessly scaring neighbors and their children," said Ron Herndon, who has fought for racial justice in Portland for four decades and led a school boycott in 1979 after the city closed predominantly black schools. "At some point, enough is enough."

Nonetheless, similar violence has continued in Portland into 2021. Antifa "celebrated" New Year's Eve 2021 by launching mortar fireworks and projectiles at law enforcement and at the Hatfield Federal Courthouse.

After two days of vandalism and violent clashes, Mayor Wheeler, a liberal Democrat, finally ended his months of appeasement by naively asking, "Why would a group of largely white, young and some middle-age men destroy the livelihood of others who are struggling to get by?" Wheeler further said it was hard for him "to accept the reality that there are just some people on this planet who are bent on criminal destruction; that there are some people who truly just want to watch the world burn." [12]

However, Wheeler still missed the central issue, that there is a longer-term goal behind the destruction and the anarchy. Call it liberal guilt, call it fear, or call it political calculation, but as with his liberal colleague Mayor Frey of Minneapolis, who we spoke about earlier, Portland Mayor Wheeler could not or would not criticize the political motives, nor the long-term goals of the protesters/rioters further to his Left.

Newly appointed Police Chief Chuck Lovell, who happens to be black, said the violence in North Portland was "offensive and hurtful" and had cost the city at least $6.2 million in overtime for its officers. [13]

In June of 2020, the Portland City Council cut nearly $16 million from the Police Bureau budget. The cuts shuttered programs like the gun violence reduction unit, as well as a youth services program, and ended the presence of school resource officers in three school districts. As the crisis continued into July, the city experienced a sharp rise in gun violence that overwhelmingly hurt black people. There were 99 shootings – more than triple the amount from the previous July – and by the end of July, the city had tallied 366 non-suicide shootings in 2020 compared to 388 in all of 2019. Roughly two-thirds of the victims in

July were black.

Further denouncing the calls to defund the police, Sgt. Derrick Foxworth, who also happens to be black, pointed out that "It's really counterproductive to having well-trained officers," adding that budget cuts always affect training first. To train, he said, there must be funding, noting that good cops cannot come from money taken away from law enforcement. [14]

Continuing the trend of black police chiefs speaking out against the radicals' demands that they resign, Detroit police Chief James Craig vowed in a Fox News interview on "The Story with Martha MacCallum," that he will not be leaving:

*"I've taken a firm stand here in Detroit and I've been supported by Detroiters. But let me just say, Detroiters want them gone. And so, I'm not leaving. They have to leave."*
(referring to groups denouncing police chiefs across the country.)

*"And I've said it publicly, both locally and nationally, and I'm going to hold my ground. Because our men and women who serve deserve much better than this."* [15]
(Detroit police Chief James Craig)

As violence heated up in Detroit and so many other cities, it became crystal clear that these were not peaceful protesters seeking to fix the system of policing. They were attempting to overthrow the system, not just of policing but also of government.

The battle lines were clearly drawn in Portland, perhaps more than anyplace else, as local police, joined by federal enforcement teams, blasted marchers with tear gas. At times, the civilians responded with weapons of their own – such as feces, bleach, bricks, or batteries. Others threw cans and bottles, shot fireworks, or pointed lasers at officers. In addition, wild mobs were seen burning American flags and Bibles, thus revealing the actual ideological basis for their protests, which had morphed into something way beyond the anti-racism theme. Despite the frequently cited descriptions in the media of peaceful protests against racism, the lawless behavior that federal officials had cited to justify their crackdown was clearly exhibited by large numbers of protesters, as was the much broader culture war that the secular leftists were hoping to achieve. [16]

The violent destruction of symbols like the American flag and the Bible shocked many Americans, who began to understand that the utter disrespect for national and religious symbols that Americans have deeply honored is indicative of an even deeper hatred of their country that such destruction indicates. Rather ironic, considering that those doing the burning were no doubt benefitting from the freedoms and tolerance that the American system provides, and that they were cynically exploiting in order to undo the system.

In the Land of Israel, we have seen such madness for years in the many violent protests against Israel. The mass demonstrations, at the Gaza border and elsewhere, are carried out by those Arabs who identify as Palestinians, sometimes joined by small amounts of leftist Israelis. These riots are identified by their terrorist organizers and sponsoring organizations as "peaceful protests against Israeli occupation," but when one examines the tactics and goals, they should be more accurately labeled as armed insurrection. In the eyes of the left-wing media that is all too eager to cast Israel as the villain, especially if the weapons used are not guns, the attackers are cast as the victims. For years Palestinian

Arab domestic terrorists have been throwing Molotov cocktails, which are easy-to-assemble gasoline bombs, at moving vehicles carrying Israeli civilians, thereby setting the cars on fire, and severely wounding, maiming, and often killing the individuals inside.

**In the Radicals' Ideology, Mothers and Daughters Become Legitimate Targets:** An Israeli policeman looks on as a vehicle burns on November 8, 2013, after Palestinians firebombed a car being driven by Jews near the community of Tekoa in Judea, southeast of Bethlehem. A mother and daughter, who were in the car at the time, were wounded in the attack.

Most of the Arabs in the Land of Israel today are descended from those who immigrated to the Land of Israel in approximately the past one hundred twenty years, moving to what the British colonialists were then calling Palestine, still using the old Roman name for the Land of Israel. The bulk of the Arab population gradually moved to the Land of Israel from the Arabian Peninsula, as the returning Jews were creating an economy and the Arabs were seeking work.

The historian Joan Peters calculated that in 1882,

**For the Revolution:** This Palestinian "struts his stuff" with the Molotov cocktail in hand and the Che Guevara shirt portraying the legendary Marxist-Leninist leader of the Cuban Marxist revolution. This reveals the strategic and ideological affinity between the various revolutionary movements.

when the Muslim Ottoman Turks ruled the territory, just the non-nomadic, settled Muslims in Palestine numbered 141,000. The Jewish population was 24,000. That was right around the time when the Jews were struggling to return home. In 1920, there were less than 500,000 Arabs living in the land, but the numbers increased in the next two decades under British rule, when Jews were restricted from returning. In those days some of the Arabs who arrived were peaceful, but many others were not, and as their numbers grew, there were acts of terrorism against Jews, but nothing as intense as the present period, when the local Arabs have been armed by naive or Israel-hating nations. In any event, few of them at that time were calling themselves Palestinians.

That semantic change came much later when it became politically beneficial to adopt a new identity as the "oppressed underdog," claiming to be the indigenous people. [17]

However, the true indigenous people were always the Jews, who had arrived in the land thousands of years earlier.

The Bible tells us of many battles between the Israelites and their enemies that were fiercely fought, but it also speaks of other battles, such as the battle of Jericho, in which God led the way, thereby making the use of weapons unnecessary. [18]

In our times, the situation has been a bit different. Molotov cocktails, or firebombs, have become one of the low-level weapons of choice for the terrorists and

**Burn the Israeli Police:** Palestinian "demonstrators" have long used Molotov cocktails, or homemade firebombs, to hit their targets, in this case, the Israeli border police.

that is what they used just outside the city of Jericho in an October 1988 terror attack on an Israeli civilian bus. Palestinian militants, Mahmud Salim Suliman Abu Khraesh of Jericho and Jum'a Ibrahim Juma Adam of Ramallah had carefully prepared their weapons. They knew what they were doing, since they had been jailed previously for attempted firebombing. As part of their preparation of the devices, they mixed glue into the gasoline, which causes the flammable liquid to stick to potential victims. Then they attacked, targeting the bus of Israeli civilians. The five fatalities included a mother and her three young children. [19] Therefore, there is no doubt that Molotov cocktails are murderous weapons, however makeshift they may seem.

Do rocks and bricks kill? Some years back, my neighbors Benny and Batsheva Shoham were driving home to Shiloh with their five-month-old baby. As they

**Murdered by a Rock Thrown at His Head:** Five-month-old baby Yehuda Shoham (of blessed memory) was but one of many Israeli civilians who have been killed by rocks thrown at their heads by Palestinian revolutionaries.

passed the village of Luban a-Sharkiya, Arabs suddenly appeared from behind a building close to the road, and as part of their peaceful protest against Israeli "occupation," hurled rocks at the car. One of those rocks smashed into the baby's head and he died of severe brain damage one week later. [20] After seeing such horrible murders, can anyone really believe that rocks are "non-lethal weapons?"

We in Israel are also familiar with such so-called non-lethal weapons like knives that have been used to kill countless Israelis in Jerusalem and elsewhere. And then there are the hundreds of exploding balloons that intentionally cause fires on impact. Those lovely multi-colored floating objects have been sent on their peaceful journeys from Hamas-controlled Gaza towards Israeli farms and villages, where they have often caused serious fire damage as part of what is called "peaceful Palestinian resistance."

Israel's approach to combatting such low-level warfare is first and foremost to define it, to recognize it for what it is – a planned, strategic, long-term war against the existing system. In Israel, the system is the State of Israel, the sovereign homeland of the Jewish people. Once we recognize that fact, we know that all aspects of Israel will be under attack, whether the attacks are violent or seemingly peaceful at times. The strategy will be to assault Israeli civilians, soldiers, educational institutions, small businesses, national parks, and forests – you name it. All become legitimate targets in the low-level war, which often is revealed as an armed insurrection.

The tactics in American cities are quite similar, with the slight exception of the arson attacks on Israel's treasured forests, which in a tiny country with limited greenery, is

**"Itbach Al Yahud!"** (Arabic for "Kill the Jews"): A rioting Palestinian in Israel gets ready to throw an already ignited Molotov cocktail at Jews.

another form of existential attack. In America, buildings are set on fire, often small businesses and commerce, which, for the political arsonists, represent the free enterprise system that conflicts with their beloved communism. That being said, their prime targets for vandalism and destruction are federal buildings, which for the anarchists have great symbolic value. If they can destroy or take over a federal courthouse, what greater symbol can there be of the weakness of law enforcement and American justice?

Most of the other low-level weapons are already being used, as well, by the Antifa and BLM activists, and they still call it peaceful protest, but only a blindly naive person would fall for such semantic gymnastics. A protest, by definition, is a strong expression of disagreement, often in large groups, but usually not violent. A riot is when a public protest becomes violent and out of control. [21] Last but not least, an insurrection is an organized attempt by a group of people to defeat their government and take control of their country, usually by violence. [22] With the exception of a few isolated peaceful marches, what we have seen increasingly in the left-wing protests has been a combination of riots and armed insurrection.

Israelis have experienced this for years from the Palestinians, whom, for many years, have been trying to undermine the sense of peace and security that Israelis strive to achieve.

When they do not have guns, they use rocks, bricks, and Molotov cocktails and they call it a "protest," but it is not. As we have discussed, bricks, rocks, and Molotov cocktails have killed and maimed thousands of Israelis.

As for groups like Antifa and Black Lives Matter and affiliated organizations that have been very active in spearheading similar such "protests", they make it very clear in their doctrine on websites, through spokespeople and elsewhere, that their goal is nothing less than the overthrow of the American system of government. They want to do to the United States what Hamas wants to do to Israel. They just have fewer guns and no missiles, yet. They also want to destroy the capitalist free market economy to be replaced by a socialist/communist system of government, and that, in addition to blatant lawlessness creating chaos, is what the looting is all about – to undo the system by destroying free enterprise.

After the demands to defund the police led, in fact, to severe cuts to police budgets, and orders by Democrat

**American Radicals - Learning from their Palestinian Comrades:** The model of low-level warfare that has long been utilized by the Palestinian terror groups against Israel is now being utilized by the radicals of the American Left as they riot in America's cities.

mayors responding to their left-wing power base caused police departments to constantly look over their shoulders before taking the necessary aggressive action against criminals, the results were seen in the streets. Looters were empowered, holders of illegal firearms were emboldened, and havoc took over in major cities like New York City and Chicago, which already were suffering from high crime rates.

In one of many incidents, on September 5, 2020, approximately 150 activists from Antifa-affiliated organizations were involved in organized violence in Manhattan, New York City.

During the protest, which was co-organized by RAM NYC and the New Afrikan Black Panther Party, activists smashed display windows at a variety of stores and banks. The rioters also called to close all police stations, and chanted, "Death to America!" as well as, "Every city, every town, burn the precinct to the ground!" as the group moved up Lafayette Street in lower Manhattan, while smashing the plate glass facades of five banks, two Starbucks cafes, and Duane-Reades Pharmacy, causing at least $100,000 in damage from Foley Square up to 24th Street.[23]

New York police arrested eight young suspects, who were found to be armed with a stun gun, smoke grenades, and graffiti supplies. One of the arrested rioters was a wealthy twenty-year-old woman, Clara Kraebber, an Upper East Side resident, whose mother is an architect and whose father is a child psychiatrist, the kind of hard-working professionals that BLM activists would accuse of having "white privilege." Some of the others were Elliot Rucka, twenty-one, of Portland, Oregon, the son of a famed comic-book writer and best-selling author, along with Claire Severine, twenty-seven, a signed model and actress who has lived in Canada and Ireland, and Adi Sragovich, twenty, from Great Neck, L.I., a student at the elite Sarah Lawrence College. The young activist lost her phone during the rowdy weekend protests and promptly called up her mother who "made arrangements" to replace the cell phone right away, her mom told The New York Post. [24] Other "comrades" were Etkar Surette, twenty-seven, who spent her summer vacations in Austria as a child and Frank Fuhrmeister, thirty, a freelance art director who has done work for Pepsi, Samsung and Glenlivet. His most recent address is a stately home on Reed Island Drive in Jacksonville, Florida's expensive Beacon Hills and Harbour neighborhoods. [25]

In fact, many of the protesters act like spoiled rich kids who feel guilty about their "white privilege," and maybe they are spoiled rich kids who are desperately looking for a cause, for real meaning in their lives. The problem is that they are looking in the wrong place. This particular phenomenon reminds one of Patty Hearst, the granddaughter of American publishing magnate William Randolph Hearst, who became internationally known for the events that followed her 1974 kidnapping by the left-wing organization, Symbionese Liberation Army.

The young woman was found and arrested nineteen months after being abducted, by which time she had become a fugitive wanted for serious crimes committed during her time as a member of the revolutionary group.

**Privileged Revolutionaries:** Many of the naive young people attending the protests, that soon become violent riots, are actually privileged kids looking for a cause. Due to that search for meaning, many have accepted the Marxist narrative as taught by their leftist college professors, along with the revolutionary romanticism, without looking at the full picture. Pictured here in mug shot after her arrest in September 1975, Patty Hearst - publishing heiress, hostage turned revolutionary, then turned ex-revolutionary. On the left, the banner of the now-extinct Symbionese Liberation Army, which she was involved with for nineteen months.

She was held in custody, and there was speculation before trial that her family's resources would enable her to avoid time in prison. She ended up having her prison time commuted to seven years and was eventually pardoned by President Bill Clinton. Whether Patty Hearst had become a voluntary member, or a violently coerced member of the Symbionese Liberation Army is still debated to this day. However, the difference is that Patty Hearst was, in fact, kidnapped by armed terrorists, while these other rich kids smashing windows, setting buildings on fire, and attacking police precincts on behalf of the current "liberation armies" do not have that excuse. [26]

The radical groups openly rationalize and justify their rioting and looting, but more and more Americans are beginning to understand that the goals of the radicals are not benign. Intentionally fighting to weaken law enforcement is part of a master plan to cause a breakdown of law and order. The problem is that weakening the police, whose job it is to protect crime-plagued communities, only increases the crime in those long-suffering communities.

*"You cannot strengthen the weak by weakening the strong."*
(Abraham Lincoln) [27]

However, the Black Lives Matter organization and the affiliated activists in the broader movement seem, at best, to be profoundly confused about who they are really helping and who they are really hurting. BLM members in Chicago held a rally on August 10, 2020, to support the more than one hundred arrested the previous night following widespread looting and rioting that caused at least $60 million in property damage and saw thirteen police officers injured, according to a report.

The rally was organized by Black Lives Matter Chicago and was held at a police station in the South Loop where organizers said that individuals were being held in custody. At least one organizer called the looting tantamount to "reparations."

*"I don't care if someone decides to loot a Gucci or a Macy's or a Nike store, because that makes sure that person eats ... That makes sure that person has clothes ... That is reparations ... Anything they wanted to take, they can take it because these businesses have insurance."*

(Ariel Atkins, a BLM organizer, according to NBC Chicago)

Black Lives Matter Chicago issued a statement obtained by the Chicago Sun-Times that read, "The mayor clearly has not learned anything since May, and she would be wise to understand that the people will keep rising up until the [Chicago Police Department] is abolished and our Black communities are fully invested in," the group said in a statement. [28]

Now that is a brilliant plan: Delete the police, thereby enabling and encouraging looting, and then, in a convoluted twisting of logic, call it reparations! Obviously, the law of the jungle carries more weight for these anarchists than the common sense of the Ten Commandments and the prohibition on stealing that has been accepted as the norm in most of the civilized world. Then again, anarchy and civilization are two concepts that don't exactly exist together in harmony.

The ramifications of such convoluted thinking led to continued rioting and looting in many American cities as the summer of 2020 came to a close, and it spread to other states, with Kenosha, Wisconsin being set on fire from random violence, massive looting, and destruction of businesses. The pretense, once again, was the killing of an armed black suspect who apparently struggled with the police while resisting arrest. In the new America, it is almost considered acceptable that a suspect will violently resist arrest, and if he gets shot in the process, the cop is always to blame, as long as the suspect is black. Such logic has put American police on the defensive, to the extent that many of them are afraid to respond to violence, knowing that they will be accused by the mainstream media and many left-wing mayors of using unnecessary force.

Stunning videos posted online have shown uniformed NYPD cops getting drenched with buckets of water by brazen young men in Harlem and Brooklyn, with one clip even showing a soaked cop getting beaned in the back of the head with an empty, red plastic bucket while the cop and his partner were trying to handcuff a suspect on the hood of a car.

*"Everybody's outraged ... It's disgusting, embarrassing. There's lawlessness around here now."*
(NYPD source)

Both videos show bucketfuls of water hurled toward cops as onlookers watch – and in some cases laugh or prance in glee. [29]

The emasculation of the American police is being interpreted by the left-wing ideologues as the dawn of their revolution, in the same way that the Palestinians rejoiced and laughed when young Israeli soldiers or police at times seemed afraid of responding to their rock attacks. Young Palestinians have a sixth sense for weakness and they pounce on any indication that law enforcement is afraid to respond strongly.

The perception of weakness is fatal when trying to combat this deadly virus of aggression and lawlessness, and it is worse than Corona, because it will not be healed so easily, not by a vaccine and not by medications.

The human psychology of low-level terror must be understood by law enforcement, but more importantly, by the politicians. As I always say, Israel is in a "very bad neighborhood" with some very bad people, and we've learned from very painful experience that insurrection is war, but there are also some very bad people in America whose intentions are no better. Only through strength, on many levels, will they be stopped.

The leftist radicals are always planning, always organizing, and this was evident in the build-up to the planned violent aftermath of the November 2020 presidential elections, in the case of a Trump victory. The radical organizers made a plan of action, revealed in a recording purportedly of one training session hosted over Zoom by the "Sunrise Movement," which featured Lisa Fithian, who has been described by Mother Jones, "as the nation's best-known protest consultant."

In the video, Fithian showed a target map displaying all the police stations, key government buildings, media outlets and buildings occupied by "Trump boosters" in the DC area. She discussed "what would it take to surround the White House."

*"We're facing an administration and a potential coup and a potential insurrection ... Is there going to be a war? Are people gonna get killed? Like is that on anybody else's mind? I'm guessing it is. We're going to see potential fighting all over the country or in some hotspots, and we've already seen that,*

*so how do we work together across the country to help support each other no matter where we are and to maximize our impact by doing similar things on similar days at similar times?"*

(Lisa Fithian)

In a call to violence and illegal action, Fithian said demonstrators willing to break windows on government buildings should go a step farther and get inside. She told those on the call:

*"We have to be willing to put our bodies on the line and take on some discomfort and sacrifice risk in order to change things ... We are going to be in a crisis but we want to make sure it's one that we are creating. We want them to be responding to us and us not responding to them.* **In a situation of a coup or an insurrection or an uprising, whoever's got the guns, often can win.** *We should be clear. Trump's gotta go."*

(Lisa Fithian, according to the recording of the call posted to the YouTube account SunriseExposed.) [30]

There can be no doubt that the year 2020 will be remembered negatively, not just because of the Corona virus craziness that emerged from Wuhan, China, and spread around the globe, but also because of the "protests." While cures and treatments are usually found for viruses, the impact of the radical Left protest movement, that has strangely captivated so many of America's millennials, will reverberate and most likely be continued and strengthened in the years to come.

It is also important to take note of the link between these two headline stories of 2020. The brutal, self-serving system of the Chinese Communist Party (CCP) has in recent years created massive pollution, numerous pandemics, and suppression of the Chinese people's will to be free, most recently in Hong Kong, as well.

The Covid-19 virus that the CCP, either irresponsibly or maliciously, unleashed on Western Civilization in 2020 has created bedlam in people's daily lives and badly damaged capitalist economies around the world.

What is most ironic, however, is that the CCP's communist/socialist system of tight governmental control of every aspect of people's lives is essentially what the American Marxist ideologues are promoting in their efforts to bring their model of change to America. The first step is to increase anarchy to further the destruction of Judeo-Christian civilization. The next step is to replace it.

## Chapter Five
# Appeasement Does Not Work

*"An appeaser is one who feeds a crocodile–hoping it will eat him last."*

(Winston Churchill) [1]

*"They who can give up essential liberty to obtain a little temporary safety deserve neither liberty nor safety."*

(Benjamin Franklin) [2]

The Munich Agreement was an agreement concluded on September 30, 1938, by Nazi Germany, the United Kingdom, the French Third Republic, and the Kingdom of Italy. It provided "cession to Germany of the Sudeten German territory" of Czechoslovakia. Most of Europe celebrated the agreement, because it prevented the war threatened by Adolf Hitler by allowing Nazi Germany's annexation of the Sudetenland, a region of western Czechoslovakia inhabited by more than three million people, mainly German speakers. Hitler announced it was his last territorial claim in Europe, and the choice seemed to be between war and appeasement.

That very same day, upon his return to Great Britain, British Prime Minister Neville Chamberlain delivered his controversial speech to crowds in London, proclaiming "peace for our time."

There are some historians who believe that the concession of allowing the Nazi annexation of the Sudetenland was actually positive, because it enabled the UK to postpone a war that it wasn't yet prepared

**The Epitome of Appeasement:** British Prime Minister Neville Chamberlain (left) and German Chancellor Adolf Hitler (in the tan jacket), leave their meeting at Bad Godesberg, September 23, 1938. Chamberlain tried to appease Hitler by giving him the Sudetenland, a chunk of disputed European territory. By showing weakness, Chamberlain didn't bring peace, but he absolutely increased the magnitude and the horror of WWII.

to win, but most are certain that the concession simply was an act of psychological weakness that strengthened Hitler in his march forward. That assessment was proven correct on March 15, 1939, when Hitler seized all of Czechoslovakia, in defiance of the promises he had given at Munich, and Prime Minister Chamberlain, who had just championed appeasement several months before, decided on a policy of resistance to further German aggression. Today, the Munich Agreement is widely regarded as a failed act of appeasement, and the term has become "a byword for the futility of appeasing expansionist totalitarian states." [3]

Likewise, the worst way to counter the revolutionary tendencies of radical groups, in America and elsewhere, is through appeasement. Appeasement is like throwing a small piece of steak to a pack of wolves. They will happily pounce on it, but then they will demand more, and the demands will grow greater every day. Every concession given to a radical hater will only bring more demands.

It would be helpful to learn from the State of Israel's worst strategic mistake in its young history as a modern nation in the Middle East combatting its own challenges from domestic terrorism. Israel's misguided use of appeasement in recent decades to ward off revolutionary challenges from the Palestinians can be highly instructive in this regard. While Israel's local enemies have greater military capability than America's domestic terrorists, the political tactics are remarkably similar. A little background will help to provide context, which in turn, will provide a better understanding of the dual strategy of radicals.

In Israel, perhaps more than anyplace else, we breathe history, archeology, and the Bible. Everything here is based on history, so that is a good place for us to start.

Israel recaptured the territories of Judea and Samaria, as well as eastern Jerusalem and the Golan Heights, among others, in the Six Day War of 1967, which was a defensive war in which the Jewish state was attacked from all sides. Despite Israel's historical roots in those territories, the Arab nations and the Palestinian terrorist organizations that had recently been established demanded that Israel surrender the land that it had just recaptured.

At the Rabat Summit of Arab nations in 1974, it was decided to adopt a dual strategy to combat Israel. The plan was to combine low-level terrorism and targeted terror attacks on Israeli civilians, along with an intense and ongoing propaganda campaign, to apply heavy pressure on potential allies around the world to view Israel as the aggressor. In the succeeding years, propaganda efforts were also made to influence the Israeli people, with a special political focus on the secular Left, which had a gradually weakening belief in the justice of the Zionist mission. Almost without exception, the more religious, more right-wing Jewish population in Israel, were Biblically grounded with a firm deeply rooted belief that the Land of Israel is Israel's divine inheritance and that the return to Israel, expressed in the reestablishment of the sovereign Jewish state, was not only a fulfillment of prophecy, but was totally justified historically.

In any event, the Arabs focused on aggressive intimidation through violence, combined with a propaganda war in cooperation with the secular Israeli Left. This was all intended to achieve the political goal of gaining concessions from the centrist Israeli politicians, thereby weakening the Jewish state. The strategy was stunningly successful. The movement in Israel to surrender the territories that had just been recaptured in a defensive war gained steam, while the pressure on Israel from the United States and Europe also grew stronger until finally, the goal of attaining political concessions from Israel started to bear fruit.

In a tragic act of appeasement in September 1993, the Oslo Accords were secretly agreed to and eventually signed by Prime Minister Yitzhak Rabin of Israel and the Palestine Liberation Organization's (PLO) Yasser Arafat in a grand ceremony on the White House lawn, overseen by US President Bill Clinton. Despite the appealing slogan that Rabin often used that "peace is made with enemies," the accompanying rise in expectations was an unmitigated disaster, which led to a sharp spike in demands for the establishment of

**Learn from Israel's Mistakes:** The Oslo Accords were believed by its enthusiastic proponents to be a way of encouraging the Palestinians towards peace by giving them some of what they wanted at first, in order to test their good intentions. They failed the test miserably, by initiating and financing twenty-five plus years of horrific terrorism against Israel. Israeli Prime Minister Yitzhak Rabin, US President Bill Clinton, and Yasser Arafat at the second celebratory Oslo Accords signing ceremony in the White House on September 28, 1995.

an independent Palestinian state in all of Judea and Samaria, with its capital in Jerusalem. The PLO and its various terrorist components were not appeased by Israel's surprising show of weakness, but frequently complained to their American and European sponsors that the Israeli surrender of territory was not happening quickly enough. In the framework of the agreement, the PLO was given seven autonomous cities in Judea, Samaria, and Gaza, and a quasi-governmental body called the Palestinian Authority (PA) was set up in those areas. The PA was headed by Arafat, and eventually by Arafat's successor, Mahmoud Abbas. The local police force that was permitted for them in those seven cities were soon developed into mini-low-level armies with massive international financial support, and the autonomous areas were also used to stash weapons and to produce homemade bombs to be used in hundreds of horrific terror attacks on Israeli civilians, including bus bombings, shootings at street cafes, Molotov cocktail attacks and rock attacks on Israeli cars, terrorist infiltrations to Jewish communities in Judea and Samaria, and shootings on the roads. When the euphoria of the Israeli Left eventually evaporated, the Oslo Accords came to be seen for what they were, an act of appeasement and betrayal of Israel's citizens that led to decades of Palestinian terrorist warfare against the Jewish state.

It's important to note that there were many terrorist attacks before 1995, but the big escalation occurred after the signing of the Oslo Accords, which allowed the Palestinian Authority to have guns. Many of those weapons made their way into the hands of their constituent terrorist organizations, so while the use of the low-level weapons continued, the access to guns certainly increased their firepower to levels that the radicals in America can only dream of at this point, but the lesson is poignant. Don't let them upgrade their access to weapons and if they somehow do, don't let the left-wing politicians look the other way as they did in Israel, because the situation will quickly spin out of control.

The terrorism in Israel has continued almost unabated since 1995, but the years 1995-2006 were the most intense, with terror attacks almost every day. At the end of the year 2001, I was badly wounded, along with my then three-year-old son in a terror shooting attack carried out by one of the main terrorist organizations sponsored by the Palestinian Authority. My son was shot in the head and I was shot in the leg. The terrorists who wounded us were eventually arrested and convicted, but to this day, they receive monthly salaries from that same PA, as do the perpetrators of thousands of other attacks on Israelis. The Oslo Accords had opened up the floodgates of international financial aid, which the PA used to fund its armed insurrection, as well as to enhance its propaganda war against Israel.

Appeasement does not work.

As part of the Oslo Accords, Israel's (left-wing dominated) media and schools made a serious and conscious effort to educate towards peace. Many objective observers have noted that Israeli educators and the media, as well as the Israel Defense Forces educational apparatus bent over backwards, even distorted the facts to show balance and understanding for the Palestinian narrative.

# B'klyn-born settler and son wounded

By Uri Dan in Jerusalem and Marsha Kranes in New York

A Brooklyn-born teacher and his [-]year-old son were wounded vhen Palestinians fired on their ar as they headed to their home n the Israeli-occupied West 3ank.

"They started shooting at us, a ot of shooting," David Rubin, 44,

said of the Monday night ambush.

One of the slugs slammed into Rubin's leg; another hit his son, Ruby, in the back of his neck, narrowly missing his spine.

The two were returning to the Jewish settlement of Shilo after a day's outing in Jerusalem when Palestinians opened fire from a passing car.

Ruby went into immediate shock and didn't answer his father's shouts.

Rubin, who was losing blood, battled pain and increasing weakness to keep driving.

When he finally reached the nearest settlement, Ofra, "he opened the car door, fell out and called for help," said Eitan, his

14-year-old stepson.

A local man rushed the Rubins to a Jerusalem hospital.

"My father is OK. He just has a hole in his leg," Eitan reported. "My brother is more serious. When we visited him yesterday, he didn't recognize me or my sisters. He only recognized my mother."

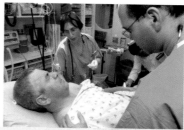

### THE JERUSALEM
# POST
www.jpost.com

VOLUME LXIX, NUMBER 21067

TUESDAY, DECEMBER 18, 2001

NIS 6.00 (EILAT NIS 5.10)

# 3 wounded in terrorist ambushes

**Shot and Wounded by Palestinian Terrorists:** The years of terrorism included a terror attack in which the author of this book was shot and wounded in a terrorist shooting attack, along with his then three-year-old son who was shot where the skull meets with the neck causing a fracture and internal bleeding in the cerebellum. The bullet missed the toddler's brain stem by one millimeter.

The Oslo II Agreement stated that:

*Israel and the (Palestinian) Council will ensure that their respective educational systems contribute to the peace between the Israeli and Palestinian peoples and to peace in the entire region, and will refrain from the introduction of any motifs that could adversely affect the process of reconciliation.* [4]

The Palestine illusion has been one of the most successful hoaxes of the twenty-first century, ranking up there with the Russia collusion hoax that figures from the Obama administration promoted to bring down President Trump, with the help of the mainstream media. The myth promoted frequently on PA television, that there once was a sovereign Arab country called Palestine is one of the great lies of our times and thousands of Jews have been murdered or wounded in its name. Many of those have been shot by armed terrorists with guns, others with the lower-level lethal weapons, but the goal has always been insurrection leading to the destruction of Israel. The following public statements were made by the PA leadership **after** the Oslo commitments to educate towards peace:

*"We welcome every drop of blood spilled in Jerusalem. This is pure blood, clean blood, blood on its way to Allah."*

(PA Chairman Mahmoud Abbas) [5]

*"I will continue my Jihad (holy war) for peace."*

(PA Founder and Abbas predecessor Yasser Arafat) [6]

For a long time, centrist Israelis had looked the other way when such contradictory statements were made, not taking them seriously and/or not wanting to take them seriously. The Israeli avoidance of reality only emboldened the Palestinian leadership, which cynically made lots of confusing, contradictory "jihad for peace" type statements. This further riled up the radical masses, thereby sending them the message that the Palestinian revolution will continue to succeed in manipulating the Israeli political system, talking peace and negotiation with one hand, while taking hostile, often violent action with the other. It took a number of years until the peace bubble burst, but it soon became clear to more and more Israelis that appeasement does not work. The number of Israelis that are still ignoring the Palestinian dual strategy has decreased sharply in recent years as the deceitful veil of peaceful protest and diplomacy has been removed, and the true hostility of Abbas and the Palestinian Authority has been exposed for most Israelis to see.

Abbas and his PA still play good cop to the bad cops from the seemingly more radical Hamas and Palestinian Islamic Jihad, but Israelis are not as gullible anymore. They are not fooled when Mahmoud Abbas announces, "days of rage," which are modeled after the BLM or Al Sharpton protests in America that are ostensibly peaceful marches, but soon become violent rampages.

In Israel, we have learned that peaceful protest is always a front for the rioting and the violence that is sure to come. It has taken almost thirty years of looking at the Middle East through rose-colored glasses, but we have reached the point that few Israelis are willing to ignore the "pay to slay" program, in which the PA gave approximately $150 million in salaries to terrorist prisoners and released prisoners just in 2019 alone. They have been doing it for years. Sometimes they call it a "social needs/social justice" program to help the families of the "heroes." Israelis know better by now, especially those of us who are direct victims of their terrorist "heroism." [7]

However, the official Palestinian Authority-controlled television, which is basically an extension of the PA educational system, has continued to educate PA children, for several decades now, that all of Israel is "Palestine," according to program translations provided by the media watchdog, Palestinian Media Watch. [8]

The appeasement policy enabled the Hamas radical terror group to promote their radical ideas on children's shows that they sponsored. On one such show, a Mickey Mouse-style character encouraged terrorism against Israel and the United States. The al-Aqsa television channel featured a show for children, called "Tomorrow's Pioneers." It was hosted by a presenter called Farfur, who dressed up in a Mickey Mouse suit and advised children to drink their milk as well as encouraging activism against the "Zionist occupation of Palestine."

In one clip which appeared on YouTube, a young viewer speaking to Farfur by telephone recited a poem which included the lines: "Rafah sings 'Oh, oh.' Its answer is an AK-47." As the poem was being read out, Farfur, the Mickey Mouse character pretended to shoot an assault rifle, while another child pointed out to Farfur:

*"It is the time of death, we will fight a war."*

Walt Disney's daughter, Diane Disney Miller, attacked the appropriation of Mickey Mouse, the comic character created in 1928 that became the Walt Disney Company's most familiar icon.

The late Ms. Miller, at that time the only surviving child of the late Walt Disney who died in 1966, told the New York Daily News:

*"Of course, I feel personal about Mickey Mouse, but it could be Barney as well. It is not just Mickey. It is indoctrinating*

You're calling us despicable terrorists, Farfour?

**Exploiting Mickey Mouse to Spread Hatred:** Education is "ground zero" in the Palestinian propaganda war and children are a prime target.

*children like this, teaching them to be evil. The world loves children, and this is just going against the grain of humanity ... What we're dealing with here is pure evil and you can't ignore that.*"[9]

In its remarkably successful public relations war against Israel, the Palestinian indoctrination of children has been central. They have learned to appeal to the young and to use the educational system well. The hatred of Israel has been deeply ingrained in the Arab youth, even if they do not understand the lies on which that hatred is based.

Similar tactics have been used for decades by left-wing radicals in the United States, and in recent years, it has been bearing fruit. Any positive mention of Christianity, Judaism, or even God is considered unacceptable in public schools, while even mild praise of the Founders has become taboo. Furthermore, the political correctness of the Left has become dominant on college campuses throughout America. Conservative activists are routinely attacked on college campuses, not just verbally, but also physically. The Left's "shutdown" strategy of forcibly, even violently preventing differing opinions from being expressed has proven to be very effective. Here are a few witness testimonies from late 2019:

*"Over the last semester, myself and the members of the Chico State Republicans have been spat on, battered, assaulted, followed around campus, sexually harassed, and even mobbed by 300 students at once. This is the kind of environment that has been created by the modern-day college campus."*

(Chico State College Republicans President Michael Curry told The College Fix.)

In mid-November at Binghamton University in New York, the school's College Republicans chapter held a table event promoting an upcoming speaking engagement with famed economist Art Laffer, the father of supply-side economics. Video emerged showing a large crowd of angry students screaming at members of the club and grabbing their materials from the table.

At the University of Michigan in October, meanwhile, a student destroyed an information table set up by the conservative student group Turning Point USA. After accusing the club of engaging in "hate speech" and ripping up the club's materials and throwing them in the trash, the student took a marker and threatened to write on one of the members of the club. After police were called, the vandal quickly left. [10]

It should be pointed out that the aggressive, intolerant behavior on college campuses is the opposite of what was once called liberalism, or the free exchange of ideas, which used to be the hallmark of college life. The Left has ceased to be liberal and has become a shutdown and cancel culture that is the antithesis of the free exchange of ideas, and that is very sad.

The National Association of Scholars posted a very relevant study by Mitchell Langbert and Sean Stevens that reviews prior research about the left-right divide on college campuses and comes to some disturbing conclusions about the biases in the American higher education system.

Langbert and Stevens examined voter registration and candidate contributions for a sample of more than 12,000 professors from several of the top schools in each state. They found that "48.4% are registered Democrats and 5.7% are registered Republicans..." Registration ratios ranged from 3:1 in economics departments to 42:1 in anthropology and tended to be worse at higher-ranked schools. In terms of donations, 2,081 professors gave exclusively to Democrats and only 22 gave exclusively to Republicans, an incredible 95:1 ratio, though the actual dollar amounts were skewed "only" 21:1. Should we be surprised that so many college students identify as Democrats or socialists? [11]

Organizations like Black Lives Matter and Antifa, while not possessing their own school systems, have sought to infuse their hateful ideology into the public school system and use it to brainwash American children about the evils of the United States of America, its "systemic racism" and its brutally racist police force. BLM and its leftist allies have created and marketed curriculums that deliver what they see as important Marxist messages about the built-in racism in the free market system, with such topics as "Gentrification, Displacement, and Anti-Blackness," [12] as if the idea of a middle-class white person looking for a good housing deal on the edge of a less upscale black neighborhood is inherently racist. And what about a middle-class black person looking for a similar deal in the same neighborhood – Is that racist as well? Of course, it is not, but if you ask that question, they will tell you that a black person cannot be racist and that closes down the discussion. Another choice topic in this curriculum for children is called "Discipline, the School-to-Prison Pipeline, and Mass Incarceration." [13]

One of the favorite targets of the thought police is the traditional family. A public school in Buffalo, N.Y. has integrated Black Lives Matter propaganda into its curriculum for elementary school children, encouraging them to question the importance of the nuclear family.

According to several lesson plans obtained by "Tucker Carlson Tonight" (Fox News), the unnamed Buffalo public school instructed students in the fourth and fifth grades to question the importance of their own family as part of a broader effort to promote a radically left-wing agenda in line with the Black Lives Matter movement.

The lesson plans prepared by the Buffalo Public Schools' Office of Culturally and Linguistically Responsive Initiatives, instructs teachers to discuss various "guiding principles" with students including "Black Villages," which they describe as "the disruption of Western nuclear family dynamics and a return to the 'collective village' that takes care of each other." [14]

In other words, the all-knowing leftist rulers will organize an alternative to the traditional family, as part of their efforts to undo Judeo-Christian civilization and its time-proven values. According to the BLM "social experts," mothers and fathers are not conducive to furthering the Marxist agenda.

Another concrete example at the school level of the pressure campaign on the educational system was recently witnessed in Baltimore. An elite private school in Baltimore, originally founded by Jews, was pressured into revamping its curriculum in response to a pressure campaign by Black Lives Matter activists demanding an examination of the school's "wealth hoarding" and "tolerance of Zionism."

According to the report, the BLM activists' latest academic target is Baltimore's Park School, which, ironically, was founded in 1912 by Jews who were barred entry into the city's existing private schools.

In a letter to the school, an anonymous group identifying itself as the "Black at Park Organizing Collective" calls for "an examination of Park's history: its inception, early exclusions, culture of whiteness and wealth hoarding, its tolerance of Zionism, and its parasitic relationship to Baltimore City." [15]

Peter Hilsee, a spokesman for the Park School, told the Free Beacon that administrators are "aware of the letter" and are speaking with its authors.

*"It would not be appropriate to provide details about our correspondence ... I can say that our school is now involved in a robust process of reshaping our diversity, equity, and inclusion initiatives, and we are steadfastly committed to confronting systemic and institutionalized racism within our walls and in our broader community."* [16]

(Peter Hilsee)

The appeasement evident in his words speak volumes

about the weakness in an educational system so lacking in values that it would allow itself to be dictated to, essentially threatened, by an organized mob of bullies. The dictated demands are in the letter, but the threat of violence is in the sponsored rioting and looting, in the arson attacks, and in the intimidation of law enforcement and the business community. Nothing further needs to be said to get the weak-kneed school administrators to comply.

The language in the letter highlights the prevalence of anti-Semitism in the radical activism on the Left. Across the country, protesters associated with the movement have defaced Jewish institutions, demanded that American Jews denounce Israel, and embraced anti-Semitic Nation of Islam leader Louis Farrakhan, who has condemned Jews, Judaism, and Israel for years. Linda Sarsour, a Palestinian American activist based in Brooklyn, has regularly incited against Israel's existence as a Jewish and democratic state, and was given great status in the radical Left movements when she served as one of the three leaders of the Women's March. Sarsour has also drawn a direct parallel between the United States' treatment of its black citizens to Israel's "racist" treatment of Palestinians. Last but not least, she has also publicly condemned Israel for American police brutality, claiming that US police were trained by their Israeli counterparts. [17]

Being anti-Israel, even anti-Semitic, has become a central doctrine of the far Left that is truly disturbing. However, what is even more troubling is the silence of the long-time Democrat Congressional leaders in the Senate and the House, Chuck Schumer and Nancy Pelosi, who have both lacked the courage to stand up to the outright anti-Israel, anti-Zionist and anti-Semitic statements of Congresswomen Rashida Tlaib and Ilhan Omar. The leadership of the Democrat Party seems to be on the run, intimidated by its extreme left-wing flank that supports every false liberation movement, but appears to have an ideologically rooted hatred of the genuine liberation movement that is called Israel, as well as Jews who don't neatly fit the intersectionality of the radical Left narrative. That is truly sad, because this is the party that was once the party of Harry Truman and other great friends of Israel, but times have changed and anti-Zionism has become fashionable for ignoramuses like Congresswoman Alexandria Ocasio-Cortez who has admitted her utter lack of knowledge about Israel and the Middle East, but nonetheless parrots the ideological line that the leftist doctrine demands. [18]

While the rioting, the lootings, and the arson attacks are certainly frightening and the violence serves as an implicit threat, it is the quiet, but persistent efforts to change the educational system that are bearing the most resilient low-hanging fruit. While we may recall the ruthless Chinese Communist dictator Mao Zedong's slogan, "Political power grows out of the barrel of a gun," the notorious, yet more pragmatic, Soviet Communist leader Vladimir Lenin has been the preferred model for the radical Left movements in the United States. For sure, he was a pragmatist only within the revolutionary framework. He was engaged in a total war which he used to justify every means he thought necessary to achieve his goals – including summary executions, concentration (re-education) camps, and the physical liquidation of entire social classes – but he understood that more "peaceful" strategies were needed

**Revolutionary Comrades:** Communist-Socialist leaders from two continents at the Bolshoi Theater in Moscow at a meeting in honor of Joseph Stalin's 70th birthday on December 21, 1949, (left to right: Chairman Mao Zedong; Armed Forces Minister Marshal Nikolai Bulganin; and Stalin).

until his Bolshevik revolution attained full power.

The American model for revolution was developed by American socialist ideologue Saul Alinsky, whose standard was "vote for us now, but when we become the government (and we have the guns), it will be a different story." This has been the credo of all modern totalitarians, including Adolf Hitler, who was elected Chancellor, but then made himself Fuhrer, after which he shut down the voting booths forever. [19]

As explained so well by American researcher and writer David Horowitz, Alinsky's advice to radicals can be summed up in the following way. Even though you are at war with the system, do not confront it as an opposing army; join it and undermine it as a fifth column

**Fighting Free Markets and Private Initiative:** The 2011 Occupy Wall Street Protests in New York City had a specifically anti-capitalism focus, anti-police passion, and a little anti-Semitism thrown in for good measure. The protests spread throughout the United States and even around the world, becoming the model for the raucous radical left demonstrations that have been seen more recently in American cities.

from within. To achieve this infiltration, you must work inside the system for the time being. Alinsky spells out exactly what this means:

*"Any revolutionary change must be preceded by a passive, affirmative, non-challenging attitude toward change among the mass of our people."*

In other words, it is first necessary to sell the people on the concept of the change itself … You do this by proposing moderate changes which open the door to your radical agendas.

*"Remember: Once you organize people around something as commonly agreed upon as pollution, then an organized people*

*is on the move. From there, it is a short and natural step to political pollution, to Pentagon pollution."*

It is not an accident that the Green Czar appointed by then President Obama to jump-start the climate change revolution was Van Jones, an Alinsky disciple and a self-described communist. [20]

The concept should be clear to all. The leftist radicals that have spearheaded the recent protest movements in America, from Occupy Wall Street and the Women's March to the George Floyd protests have seized upon issues like police brutality and climate change to galvanize the often naive left-leaning masses out into the streets, and they have done so successfully. However, the sustainable long-term change is happening through the radical Left's increasing influence from within the mainstream Democratic party, as well as its infiltration of the educational system at all levels.

Appeasing those who have a clear, but radical agenda would be suicidal for the United States. For that reason, President Trump's refusal to pander to that agenda during his one term as president was, indeed, admirable. One prime example was his determination, in the few years that he had in office, to build a wall along the southern border of the United States to prevent illegal immigration from/through Mexico. He rightly understood that the open border policy was part of the Left's partisan plan to change the demographic makeup of the United States by allowing the immigration of lawless individuals who would forever be indebted to them through the ballot box. As with the lawless Democrat policy of "sanctuary cities," Trump refused to give in and pushed the project forward, completing 400 miles of the powerful steel barrier by the end of October 2020.

Israel knows about the importance of walls in maintaining national integrity and security. The story of its southern border wall is highly instructive. From 2010-2012, 55,000 immigrants entered Israel illegally, an enormous amount for a country the size of New Jersey. Most of those illegals settled in South Tel Aviv, a working class, somewhat rundown neighborhood. With the unnatural infusion of thousands of illegals from Sudan and Eritrea, street crime skyrocketed, prompting grassroots pressure on the Israeli government from the local residents of South Tel Aviv and other infested towns. In response to this very real plea for help, the Israeli government decided to build a massive high-tech

**Welcoming Only Legal Immigrants:** Israel's southern border with Egypt was a porous mess, until a high-tech physical barrier was built on the entire length of the border, thereby completely halting the illegal immigration from African countries like Sudan and Eritrea. On the other hand, the totally legal immigration of 100,000 immigrants from Ethiopia was not just encouraged, but their successful absorption was supported by the entire Israeli population as a national high-priority project. A country has a right to choose its immigrants and to refuse those it deems undesirable.

steel barrier, extending the full length of the southern border between Israel and Egypt. The wall/fence was completed by the end of 2015. In 2016, only eleven illegal immigrants succeeded in entering Israel through that southern border. Then the height was raised slightly and since that time, there has been **zero** illegal entry from that border. [21]

Having halted the illegal African immigration, most of the efforts have focused on returning the illegals to their countries of origin. This has been happening in cooperation with the governments of those countries.

There were many on the Israeli Left who protested this "racist" policy with street demonstrations and pressure on left-wing lawmakers to allow the intruders to remain, but despite the almost irresistible appeal of potentially having thousands of new voters for the Left, those protests eventually dried up. [22] The fact is, that the general public was happy with the noticeable reduction in the crime rates, so it no longer was a winning issue for the Left, which cannot win without attracting votes from the independents in the center of the political map. Independents don't like street crime.

It may seem that the radicals who have worked through political channels to have open borders, as well as those who have worked behind the scenes to successfully transform the educational system have all operated according to the Alinsky model of quiet but radical change, while those who are currently creating havoc in America's cities have crossed the lines that Alinsky described, but it is really just a question of timing, or two tracks working simultaneously, each according to its capabilities at any given time. However, nothing is happening spontaneously. According to the

Alinsky model, once the Left has the ability to use the more violent means, those means are acceptable, but aggressively working within the current political and educational systems to gradually take control is the more pragmatic approach, which is ongoing. [23]

To appease such a determined, ideological movement would be a fatal mistake that would make matters far worse. They would pocket every gain and demand more, as is already happening with the defunding of police departments and the subsequent demands to completely dismantle them.

In his quest to be elected president, Joe Biden often presented himself as a relative moderate, but he will likely be reduced to a figurehead in the hands of the determined radicals in his increasingly radicalized party that will pull him further and further to the left. Once the Marxists attain significant electoral power on the national level, the proverbial wolves will pounce on the steak and demand more. And then it will be too late...

*Chapter Six*
# History Matters

*"[Israel is digging under the Temple Mount in order] to show a fabricated heritage that might help them to deceive foreign visitors into believing Jerusalem is a historical place of the Jews."*

(Sheikh Mohammad Hussein, al-Aqsa Foundation Director) [1]

*"Who controls the past controls the future. Who controls the present controls the past."*

(George Orwell, from his book, "1984") [2]

The history of Jerusalem for the Jewish people has been recorded for eternity throughout the Bible and other Jewish sources passed down from generation to generation, as well as in the writings of the great historian Josephus, who lived at the time of the great destruction of Jerusalem, some 2,000 years ago. For that reason, it is indeed incredible to read the words of the Muslim leader quoted above, who actually claims that the Temple never stood on the Temple Mount. I guess he would also claim, as radical Muslims often do, that the Jews never lived in Judea, and that Abraham, Moses, and even Jesus were Muslims, thousands, and hundreds of years before the founding of Islam.

Monuments to the past are important, even if the past reflects things that were not to our liking. The period of time when the Greeks had usurped control in Jerusalem was a traumatic period for the people of Israel and the Greeks were our enemies at that time. In fact, the story of Chanukah is about the battle against the Greeks and their local allies, and the rededication of the Temple service according to Jewish tradition. If the sad period of Greek control bothers us, should the plaque in the photo below be vandalized and/or destroyed because it was inscribed and set up by the Greeks?

**Jerusalem Temple Warning:** The plaque was inscribed (in Greek) during the late Second Temple period, during the period when the Greeks were dominant. Translation – "Let no foreigner enter within the parapet and the partition which surrounds the Temple precincts. Anyone caught [violating] will be held accountable for his ensuing death."

**Blowing the Great Trumpet:** A stone plaque with Hebrew language inscription "To the Trumpeting Place", excavated by Benjamin Mazar at the southern foot of the Temple Mount. It is believed to have been a directional sign for the priests (Cohanim, in Hebrew) who blew a trumpet announcing the beginning and the end of the Sabbath in the Second Temple.

From this, we can understand that learning history is important and learning it accurately is even more important. Revisionist history is dangerous. What is happening in the USA today is witness to that phenomenon, as the radical Left seeks to transform and redefine America by revising its history. If they are allowed to do so, all will be lost.

*"Every record has been destroyed or falsified, every book rewritten, every picture has been repainted, every statue and street building has been renamed, every date has been altered. And the process is continuing day by day and minute by minute. History has stopped."*

(George Orwell, from his book, "1984") [3]

This world as we know it has seen many powerful civilizations come and go, many leaving behind both enormous accomplishments and growth, while others have left behind great destruction – some have built legacies of greatness, and others, legacies of hatred. Many of these nations had leaders that were known for their charisma, sometimes for their charm, sometimes for their visions and creative energy and often for their valor, but there were few great ones who did not have flaws. Then there were the truly evil ones, like Adolf Hitler and Joseph Stalin, whose mass murder, anti-Semitism, and other negative accomplishments far outweighed whatever positive things they may have seemed to achieve for their countries.

By learning about all of these leaders, we begin to understand that history matters in a big way. Great leaders have always recognized that a civilization is sustained by its heritage and by the symbols that are created to commemorate its heritage, so that important historical lessons will be learned by future generations.

**Freeing the Slaves:** President Abraham Lincoln is seen here, together with key members of his Cabinet, at the first reading of the Emancipation Proclamation, which changed the legal status under federal law of more than 3.5 million enslaved African Americans in the secessionist Confederate states from enslaved to free.

It certainly is not the symbols themselves that are the civilization, but they do, indeed, represent valuable concepts, and therefore, those who want to overthrow the civilization often start by destroying the symbols and controlling the national semantics.

According to a recently released working paper drawn up by the San Francisco school district's Names Advisory Committee, Presidents George Washington, Thomas Jefferson, Abraham Lincoln, and Franklin Roosevelt all may soon have their names removed from San Francisco schools. The rationale for removing the names of Washington and Jefferson is that they owned slaves, despite the great things that they both did for their country, and despite the fact that the use of slaves was

**From the Plantation to the Senate:** After Emancipation, the process of change was gradual, but significant, at least in the northern states. This lithograph shows plantation scenes, along with portraits of former plantation slaves who became members of the United States Senate, including Benjamin S. Turner, Rev. Richard Allen, H.R. Revels, Frederick Douglass, Josiah T. Walls, Joseph H. Rainy, and William Wells Brown.

quite common at that time worldwide, as we will soon discuss. However, why Lincoln, the Great Emancipator, and why FDR, the liberal icon and creator of the New Deal? [4]

In Denver, a similar process is underway with similar rationales. Jefferson and Washington's names would be removed from schools because of the slave owner issue. As for Honest Abe? His "crime" was pointed out by school board member Tay Anderson, who noted Lincoln's words in a letter to Horace Greeley in August 1862, suggesting that he might have considered not freeing slaves if it meant preserving the Union. By that time, Lincoln had already started drafting the Emancipation Proclamation. [5]

In other words, Lincoln suddenly loses his greatness for doing what every responsible leader would do – considering the full ramifications of a potential momentous action.

The concept of "political correctness" as imposed by the American Left, along with its "cancel culture" war, did not begin in the year 2020 in American cities in the midst of the Covid-19 health crisis. It did not begin with George Floyd and the defund the police movement, nor with the renaming of schools that had been named after American heroes, nor did it begin with the tearing down of the monuments of American heroes in the Spring and Summer of 2020.

Those recent phenomena have been a dramatically disturbing outward expression of a much deeper malaise that has been afflicting American society since the anger that emerged in the 1960s in the guise of peace and love. The widespread vandalism of national monuments honoring national heroes such as George Washington,

**Is Mount Rushmore Next?** Monuments to great American heroes, including George Washington, Abraham Lincoln, Theodore Roosevelt, and Thomas Jefferson have been vandalized by the radical leftist vandals. By ignoring the great accomplishments of these leaders and ignoring global context, the message of the radicals is clear: The United States has a history that no American should be proud of.

Abraham Lincoln, Benjamin Franklin, and Theodore Roosevelt is a rebellion against the values that made America great. These great leaders, each in his own way, exemplified American greatness. For example, Franklin was a ground-breaking philosopher and scientist, who was a symbol of American creative thinking, initiative, and the quest for improvement.

*"Search others for their virtues, thy self for thy vices."*

(Benjamin Franklin) [6]

**He Believed in America and its Anti-Slavery Document, the Constitution:** Frederick Douglass, a former slave, understood that if one truly cares about the Constitution and American unity, which he fervently did, that peaceful evolution is much more stable and positive than violent revolution. When radical abolitionists, under the motto "No Union with Slaveholders," criticized Douglass's willingness to engage in dialogue with slave owners, he replied: "I would unite with anybody to do right and with nobody to do wrong." [7]

*"Don't throw stones at your neighbors, if your own windows are glass."*

(Benjamin Franklin) [8]

The destruction and/or forced removal of American heroes' monuments and remembrance is a rebellion against American exceptionalism, the concept that the United States has been a world leader because of the great Judeo-Christian values that provided its moral strength, which in turn gave it the ability to grow, to build on what was already great, and yes, to correct its flaws by fixing what needed fixing when the opportunities were created.

In an earlier chapter, we referred to a Jewish concept, known in its fullest Hebrew expression as "Tikun Olam B'Malchut Shaddai", or "Repairing the World in God's Kingdom". This concept is central in Judaism and the roots of the concept can be traced all the way back to the creation of the world.

*Thus, the heaven and the earth were finished and all their hosts. And by the seventh day, God completed His work which He had done, and He abstained on the seventh day from all His work which He had done. God blessed the seventh day and sanctified it, because on it, He abstained from all His work which God created to make.*

(Genesis 2:1-3)

A basic premise of faith-based Biblical scholarship is the idea that there are no redundant words or expressions in the Torah.

If so, why does the last line in the above verse follow the words *which God created* – with – *to make*? Aren't they synonyms?

The answer to that question can be found in the words of Rabbi Joseph B. Soloveitchik, who analyzes various commentaries about the elaborate Genesis story. Rabbi Soloveitchik points out that Biblical commentators have asked numerous questions regarding the reasons for the nature and style of the Creation story, including questions which delve into its chronology and/or its literal meaning. Soloveitchik makes it clear that, based on those discussions, one can derive many hidden lessons for humanity, which are intended to guide us as we seek an understanding of the deeper meaning of life. He explains that there are two kinds of creations: God can and often does create *yesh me'ayn* (ex nihilo – something from nothing), whereas man can only create *yesh me'yesh* (something from something).

Nonetheless, that does not diminish its importance. The words *God created* are referring to God's initial

**Explained Judaism's Moral Vision:** Rabbi Joseph B. Soloveitchik, leading rabbi of American and world Jewry, aside from being a noted authority on Jewish jurisprudence, was also a brilliant philosopher who often emphasized the moral and ethical aspects of Judaism.

creation. The words *to make* are referring to our task, of continuing and perfecting the imperfect world that God intentionally created that way. [9]

In other words, God gave us the task of continuing the process of creation to make the world a better place. In short, idealism is a central part of God's plan. Therefore, the concept of Tikun Olam has to be understood properly, if we are to also understand the process of self-correction that the United States has experienced throughout its history, and which the America haters do not want to discuss.

The 1619 Project, which describes itself as "an

ongoing initiative of The New York Times Magazine," represents a concerted effort to revise history to fit the modern social justice narrative and insert works of fiction into the educational system. [10]

Such an obsessive approach focused on the "America is systemically racist" narrative ignores the need to understand America's perceived flaws in context. Slavery, for example was not invented by the United States of America. So where and when did it all begin? Let's follow the historical context chain of events.

It has been reported that slavery first appeared, in Mesopotamia thousands of years ago. Enemies captured in war were commonly kept by the conquering country as slaves.

In the 1700s BCE, the Egyptian Pharaohs enslaved the Israelites, as is recorded in the Bible (Exodus Chapter 21). In fact, the Passover holiday specifically commemorates the Jewish people's emancipation from slavery in Egypt and is an integral part of the Jewish consciousness to this day. Later, the pagan Greeks participated in slavery, as ancient Sparta as well as Athens relied fully on the slave labor of captives.

Then there were the Romans. According to historian Mark Cartwright, "slavery was an ever-present feature of the Roman world," in which "as many as one in three of the population in Italy or one in five across the empire were slaves, and upon this foundation of forced labor was built the entire edifice of the Roman state and society."

By the 8th century, African slaves were being sold to Arab households in a Muslim-dominated world that, at that time, spanned from Spain to Persia.

By the year 1000, slavery had become common in England's rural, agricultural economy, with the poor

**Moses of Her People:** Harriet Tubman was an escaped slave who became "conductor" of the Underground Railroad, leading enslaved people to freedom before the Civil War. She was also a nurse, a Union spy and a women's suffrage supporter. She led people to the northern free states and Canada. This helped her to gain the name "Moses of Her People", referring of course to the Israelite leader who led the Jews in their liberation from slavery in Egypt.

yoking themselves to their landowners through a form of debt bondage. At about the same time, the number of slaves captured in Germany grew so large that their nationality became the generic term for "slaves"– Slavs.

As for the Atlantic slave trade, this began in 1444, when Portuguese traders brought the first large number of slaves from Africa to Europe. Eighty-two years later (1526), Spanish explorers brought the first African slaves to settlements in what would become the United States – a fact the New York Times gets wrong (in its own research). The Times likewise fails to mention that the

Native American Cherokee Nation also held African slaves, and even sided with the Confederacy during the Civil War. But the antipathy of many Americans toward slavery became evident as early as 1775, when Quakers in Pennsylvania set up the first abolitionist society. [11]

In fact, it is quite ironic that Betsy Ross, whose American flag was deemed politically incorrect recently by Nike, was herself both a Quaker and an abolitionist. The abrupt cancellation of the Nike American flag advertising campaign came after Colin Kaepernick, the former National Football League quarterback and "social justice" activist who started the movement to kneel during the playing of the National Anthem, privately criticized the design to Nike, according to a person with knowledge of the interaction. Kaepernick, who had signed a lucrative deal to serve as a Nike brand ambassador, expressed his concern to the company that the Betsy Ross flag had been "co-opted by groups espousing racist ideologies," the person said. [12]

For the crime of having lived in an era when the injustice of slavery was still the norm worldwide, Betsy Ross, the abolitionist, is somehow, by extension perhaps, falsely labeled a racist. Quite bizarre it is, as well as the polar opposite of historical accuracy. The pressure of radicals in defiance of historical truth wins out again and again, and that's why it's critical for everyone else to know the real history, in order to see through the distortions.

In 1780, Massachusetts became the first state to abolish slavery in its constitution. Seven years after that (1787) the US Congress passed the Northwest Ordinance of 1787, outlawing slavery in the Northwest Territories.

In 1803, Denmark-Norway became the first country in Europe to ban the African slave trade. In 1807,

**Betsy Ross, Abolitionist and American Hero:** In this vintage illustration, Betsy Ross shows Gen. George Washington (seated, left), Robert Morris and George Ross how she cut the revised five-pointed stars for the flag. Despite her artistic vision and effort on behalf of the nation in its infancy, she recently became a posthumous victim of the cancel culture, via Nike and former NFL football player Colin Kaepernick's "social justice" campaign.

"three weeks before Britain abolished the Atlantic slave trade, President Jefferson signed a law prohibiting 'the importation of slaves into any port or place within the jurisdiction of the United States.'" Jefferson's actions followed Article I, Section 9 of the Constitution.

In 1820, Spain abolished the slave trade south of the Equator, but preserved it in Cuba until 1888.

In 1834, the Abolition Act abolished slavery throughout the British Empire, including British colonies in North America. In 1847, France would abolish slavery in all its colonies. Brazil followed in 1850.

This process continued in 1863, when President

Abraham Lincoln, whose memorials in Washington, Buffalo, and elsewhere, were vandalized by left-wing "anti-racism protestors" in 2020, issued the Emancipation Proclamation, freeing all US slaves in states that had seceded from the Union, except those in Confederate areas already controlled by the Union army. This was followed in 1865 by the 13th Amendment to the US Constitution, outlawing slavery in the entire United States of America.

The most shocking dark spot in this worldwide progress in the 20th century was during the Holocaust, when the German Nazis used slave labor in industry. Up to nine million people, mostly Jews, were forced to work to absolute exhaustion – and then were sent to concentration camps, where slave labor was continued until millions were exterminated, six million of whom were Jews.

The 20th century would see emancipation finally come to Sierra Leone, Saudi Arabia, India, Yemen, and most other Muslim countries.

On the other hand, in 1954, China began allowing prisoners to be used for labor in the Laogai prison camps, thus actually reversing the emancipation process.

The last country to abolish slavery, in 1981, was Mauritania (1981), but in 1989, the National Islamic Front took over the government of Sudan and then armed new militias to raid villages, capturing and enslaving inhabitants.

Sadly, the 21st century has not rid itself totally of slavery. In fact, in 2017, a research consortium including the UN International Labor Organization, the group "Walk Free," and the UN International Organization for Migration released a combined global study indicating

**Holocaust Slave Labor, Then Death:** Jews who had been used for slave labor in Neunburg, Germany now lying slaughtered on the forest floor with a soldier standing over them.

that 40 million people are still trapped in modern forms of slavery worldwide. [13]

Despite the fact that unofficial slavery still exists in parts of the world today, it must be stated clearly that the United States followed the gradual worldwide trend in the abolition of slavery. And while it's true that full civil rights in the South were not extended until almost one hundred years later, it is an absolute falsehood to state, as many do these days, that the USA was responsible for the slave trade, although it is true that it did not buck the norm at a time when slavery was widespread. Then again, few nations did, so to single out the United States for what was, indeed, a worldwide moral stain seems to be unfair.

The absence of context is a fatal error for anyone who truly wants to understand history. If a president or future president had slaves in a time when most countries in the world had slaves, it should not be shocking, nor does it make them inherently bad as individuals. There were flaws in the world's moral system that needed to be corrected and eventually most of them were, at least in Western Civilization.

The United States underwent a long process of strengthening and improving the expression of its moral values, many of which served as a beacon to the world, already in colonial times. These lofty values, which the Founders exalted as inalienable rights that come from God, such as freedom of speech, freedom of religion, and the right to own property, were groundbreaking at that time, and even now. Through the years, Americans, often at the initiative and encouragement of peaceful grassroots movements exercising those freedoms, have worked to fix the shortcomings that needed fixing, like ending slavery, extending full civil rights to all, and providing for women's voting rights. The Jewish concept of Tikun Olam, that faults of a person or nation can be corrected, and therefore, can be redeemed through those actions, does not seem to be comprehended by the current version of the Left, which seems determined to go for the jugular, mercilessly attacking American heroes to score political points and create chaos, while carelessly, or intentionally, ignoring historical context. In their eyes, everything must be purged a la Stalin, including the symbols that represent the history of the American nation.

The political doctrine of the Left, whether it is the identity politics, the extreme emphasis on ethnic, racial,

**The Struggle for Civil Rights:** Systemic Racism eventually ended with the Civil Rights Act of 1964, but the road from emancipation to full equal rights was a long and difficult 100-year process. Actress Cicely Tyson is seen here playing a former slave in the film, "The Autobiography of Miss Jane Pittman", drinking from a segregated water fountain marked "White Only".

religious, and gender politics that divide people, or whether the goal is an outright revolution against some sort of perceived systemic evil that they believe defines America, there is no escaping their conclusion that America is inherently bad, and therefore, its heroes were also very bad. They ignore all of the good that American heroes did in their lives, since such great achievements do not neatly fit the "America is bad" narrative. Furthermore, if you disagree with this narrative, then you are also bad, and a terrible racist to boot.

From a Jewish, or Israeli perspective, there are two very basic flaws in this philosophical construct. Firstly, no person is perfect. However, every person can be redeemed from his mistakes, because God is merciful, and therefore, we should try to be merciful, as well. Secondly, there is another concept from Jewish wisdom, which we learn from the first Chief Rabbi of Israel, Rabbi Avraham Yitzhak Kook, that speaks of "Hakarat Hatov," meaning appreciating the good. Showing an awareness of, and an appreciation for the good that is done for us is a fundamental concept in Judaism. Therefore, when we read about national heroes, we need to show our appreciation for their great accomplishments, even if some serious mistakes were made along the way. [14]

King David, a great hero by anyone's standards, was the leader of ancient Israel, a great warrior, a spiritual leader who authored the Psalms, a great poet, and a great musician. He was also known for some of his moral failings, which we learn about in the Torah, and his mistakes are pointed out for us to learn from. Nonetheless, monuments built in his honor or named in his memory have not been destroyed. Institutions named for him have not had their names changed.

King Solomon was a great hero of Israel, known for his great wisdom, who built the Holy Temple in Jerusalem during his reign. He was also known for some moral failings, especially near the end of his reign. His mistakes are written about in the Torah, and we are supposed to learn from them. However, monuments built or named in his memory have not been destroyed. Likewise, institutions named for him have not had their names changed.

In modern times, as well, leaders in Israel have had their flaws. Theodor Herzl was the great visionary who took the prophetic Zionist vision of return to the Land of Israel and turned it into a political, secular movement. The purpose was to create a modern nation-state, thereby normalizing the Jewish existence and eliminating anti-Semitism by creating a "nation like all the other nations." Many religious Jews, even though they believed in fulfilling the prophetic vision of return, abhorred Herzl's rabid secularism and Judaic ignorance in his vision to create a state for the Jews, rather than a Jewish state. Even so, no Israelis have set the Mt. Herzl Military Cemetery on fire, nor have they vandalized its national monuments.

The first prime minister of the State of Israel, David Ben-Gurion was a passionate secularist who played a major role in rebuilding the Land of Israel and establishing its national institutions. However, the sad truth is that under his leadership, devoutly religious Yemenite Jewish immigrants were forced to live in strictly secular agricultural communities, and to attend secular schools, a crime that to this day, many religious Jews consider unforgivable. Despite that, and despite his reported intolerance towards many Israelis who disagreed with him, no monuments honoring Ben-Gurion have been destroyed and no attempts have been made to change the name of Ben-Gurion International Airport. [15]

So too, the immigration of Ethiopian Jews hasn't been without its challenges. Since 1980, Israel has totally financed the immigration and absorption of over 100,000 Ethiopian immigrants as a national project. Given the third-world poverty that they came from, it hasn't always been clear sailing, and, as with the much earlier Yemenite arrivals, mistakes were made, but Israel is committed to the successful absorption of all of its immigrant communities. Therefore, the focus is as it should be, not on who is to blame for mistakes, but rather to emphasize the many success stories, while trying to learn from the mistakes and moving forward. (16)

Rabbi A.Y. Kook's son, Rabbi Tzvi Yehuda Kook, refers to an interesting passage in the Zohar, a foundational work of Jewish mystical thought known as Kabbalah, with great lessons for life. The Zohar, says Rabbi Tzvi Yehuda, refers to a heavenly yeshiva (or Bible college) that one can get accepted to in the afterlife. What are its acceptance requirements? The "applicant" must be able to transform darkness into light and bitterness into sweetness – in this world! Even one

**Operation Magic Carpet:** Yemenite Jewish immigrants learn Hebrew after arrival in Israel in 1949. The term may also refer to the descendants of the Yemenite Jewish community. Between June 1949 and September 1950, the overwhelming majority of Yemen's Jewish population was transported to Israel in Operation Magic Carpet. After several waves of persecution throughout Yemen, most Yemenite Jews now live in Israel and have been successful in all realms of Israeli society.

who has committed crimes is redeemable, especially if the mistakes are recognized and corrected. Such a person can then reach great heights, because that is the essence of our task in this imperfect world, to take the evil and transform it into good. Nothing is greater than that. [17]

The same guidelines should apply to American heroes, who have been so maligned recently in the media, in the schools, and in the streets. It is so easy to criticize flaws, especially when taken out of context, but when was the last time we focused on the positive? When, in fact, was the last time that we heard about the great self-sacrifice

**Rejoining the People of Israel:** Over 100,000 Ethiopian Jews have been welcomed to Israel in recent years and some 150,000 children of those legal immigrants are now native Israelis. The young men in this photo are seen at a makeshift synagogue in Gondar, Ethiopia shortly before their arrival in Israel.

of George Washington, who willingly abandoned what many of his present-day critics would call a life of "white privilege?"

Washington was actually extremely wealthy at the age of forty-three when he took command of the Continental Army in 1775 to fight for America's independence against the most powerful army in the world. He owned 7,600 acres of land in Virginia, had a beautiful home in Mount Vernon, and in today's dollars was worth roughly $580 million. In short, he had nothing to gain and everything to lose by taking on the overwhelming task of leading what was then a rag-tag army against the British, but because he believed so deeply in the founding principles of this embryonic republic, he was willing to sacrifice it all. [18]

General Washington voluntarily served without pay in duty to his country for the entire duration of the eight-year Revolutionary War. All of the events hosted during the Revolution by the Commander-in-Chief such as celebrations and parties were also missing from the tab because they were financed through lotteries and ticket sales for admission by Washington himself. Washington never once took advantage of the country's scarce public finances to enjoy the privileges and spoils that normally come with such prominent positions of power at the soon-to-be nation's expense.

Not only did Washington provide his services as general without any salary, he also sacrificed his own financial well-being for the cause of the nation. Like many of his men, he owned a business that could not operate efficiently in his absence. In addition, uncontrolled inflation had significantly depreciated the value of the continental dollar. By the war's end, his net worth was rendered to be approximately half of what it was when the war began eight years earlier in 1775. To better put this financial sacrifice in perspective, today a five-star general makes $180,000 a year and the president of the United States makes $400,000 a year (neither figures include the allowance for travel and accommodation). [19]

Unlike today's leaders, while commanding the revolutionary war, Washington didn't have the luxury of vacation and instead endured the freezing winter conditions together with his soldiers year after year in Continental Army encampments such as Trenton, Valley Forge, Morristown and the like without the faintest prospect of victory in sight. During these uncertain times Washington administered the war on-site from these winter military barracks; working tirelessly to acquire any piece of sustenance imaginable to ensure that his army would survive, living to fight another day. [20]

In addition to being the Commander-in-Chief, Washington was the unofficial fundraiser-in-chief, convincing his close friend Hayim Solomon, the Polish-born Jewish-American financier to sustain the struggling army in its uphill war against the world's most powerful military, to the tune of $800,000, technically given as a loan, but the sum was never repaid. In today's market, that would be equivalent to a donation of approximately $40 billion. [21]

Washington could have chosen to remain on his substantial farm and in his mansion. He could have let someone else do the job. He had nothing to gain by bearing the bitter cold at Valley Forge with his men, hundreds of whom died of disease. When he was not stationed with his soldiers, he commuted on his white

**Financier of the American Revolution:** Hayim Solomon, the humble Polish-Jewish friend of General Washington, gave the equivalent of what would today be $40 billion to the struggling Continental Army for the fight against the powerful British military forces. Solomon epitomized one of the ideal personality traits praised in the Jewish "Ethics of the Fathers" book of wisdom – "Say little, Do a lot."

horse traveling from city to city in the freezing cold to gather supplies for the starving army. All of his hardship, perseverance and leadership came at the total fiscal cost of $0 dollars to the soon-to-be nation's citizens, as Washington refused to accept any pay for his service to the United States of America.

A war hero in those days could be expected to demand the kingship of a fledgling nation, but not Washington. After finally achieving victory, he announced that he was retiring from public service. On December 19, 1783, Washington handed the president of the Continental Congress Thomas Mifflin his formal resignation from the military and public service. It was not until 1789, that he was drafted back to service, to save a bankrupt and failing nation as the nation's first president. [22]

*"I had rather be on my farm than be emperor of the world."*
(George Washington) [23]

That is patriotism. It's also self-sacrifice. Such amazing dedication to the cause is something that the pampered left-wing radicals and the selfish looters rioting today in the streets of American cities know nothing about. Perhaps if they could be transported back in time and forced to serve in the freezing cold with the under-equipped Continental Army led by General Washington, they might begin to fathom the true meaning of self-sacrifice, as exhibited by the Founding Father of the American nation, whose name they want to remove from public monuments and institutions.

**Visiting the Troops:** George Washington, Commander-in-Chief of the Continental Army, visits wounded soldiers at Valley Forge. The soldiers were stationed at that time in the freezing cold of Valley Forge over the winter of 1777-1778, during the American Revolution.

## Chapter Seven
# Changing Semantics Ignoring Facts

*"All our work, our whole life is a matter of semantics, because words are the tools with which we work, the material out of which laws are made, out of which the Constitution was written. Everything depends on our understanding of them."*

(Felix Frankfurter, US Supreme Court Justice) [1]

*"We are getting into semantics again. If we use words, there is a very grave danger they will be misinterpreted. "*

(HR Haldeman, White House Chief of Staff – being questioned in Watergate Scandal) [2]

I t certainly makes sense that a Supreme Court justice, as well as a government official being questioned under oath would understand, each in his own way, of course, that words can be used to distort the public perception of objective truth. This strategy has been used by radicals remarkably well in our times. In fact, two groups have excelled at it better than most – the Muslim radical ideologues and the American leftists.

There are several steps in their carefully calculated efforts:

1.  Change the terms to "change the public perception of reality."
2.  Insist on the use of the new terms.
3.  "Call out" and attach a negative, insulting label to anyone who does not agree with the new terminology.

The late US Senator Daniel Patrick Moynihan (D-NY), who served in Congress for over two decades, was also a noted sociologist who courageously addressed some key issues that many of his fellow politicians carefully avoided. He was not afraid of pointing out the cynical use of semantics by the Left. As he explained, "Simply put, semantic infiltration is the process whereby we come to adopt the language of our adversaries in describing political reality." [3]

In other words, by immediately accepting the word distortions that are dictated to us, we are allowing the aggressors to dictate the narrative that is being implied by the new terminology.

**A Thinker's Thinker:** Senator Daniel Patrick Moynihan (D-NY) was a courageous politician and iconoclast who was not afraid of pointing out the cynical use of semantics by the Left. Little did he know (or maybe he did know) that the semantic war of the Left would reach such an extreme level of thought control.

Addressing the topic of semantic distortion before a Congressional advisory committee, Moynihan pointed out the co-opting of the term "liberation" by advocates for Communism. He noted that, "The most brutal totalitarian regimes in the world call themselves 'liberation movements.' It is perfectly predictable that they should misuse words to conceal their real nature. But must we aid them in that effort by repeating those words? Worse, do we begin to influence our own perceptions by using them?" [4]

Moynihan was not only pointing out that it is wrong to allow incorrect use of terminology, but that the incorrect use of terminology can actually falsify our understanding of that reality, thereby coercing us into believing a non-factual view of reality or history.

We have seen this recently in quite a few instances in the Left-Right political divide, which we will soon discuss, but it actually started way before that in the Middle East, when one of the first recorded cases of Semantic Deception was initiated with the establishment of the term "Palestine." While a derivative of the name Palestine first appears in Greek literature in the 5th century BCE, when the historian Herodotus called the area "Palaistine," naming it after another enemy of Israel, the Philistines (of Goliath infamy), the significant "name change" was implemented by the Roman conquerors in the second century CE. After the Romans crushed the revolt of Shimon Bar Kokhba (132 CE), which had attempted to restore the Land of Israel (specifically Jerusalem and Judea) to Jewish rule, and in fact succeeded for three years, the Roman Emperor Hadrian renamed it Palaestina in an attempt to minimize Jewish identification with the Land of Israel. [5]

Subsequently, most of the remaining Jews were exiled from their homeland.

The semantic sleight-of-hand was politically successful, probably way beyond expectations, as the name Palestine was adopted in various forms by the assortment of conquerors and empires that ruled in the Land of Israel for the next 1,808 years, until the establishment of the State of Israel in 1948. The original, and perhaps subsequent, purpose was to delete Israel from the map, but that goal was only partially accomplished, because during the long years of exile, the Jews maintained their faith, increasingly individualizing their observance, but never severing their connection to the Land of Israel. Throughout the years of exile, whenever a Jew prayed outside of the Land of Israel anywhere in the world, he prayed facing the Land of Israel – always. And that has not changed, even today.

Then, of course there is the misuse of the word "liberation" that Senator Moynihan had referred to when citing totalitarian regimes, but the term has been used by the Arabs since 1964, when they established the Palestine Liberation Organization, with the stated goal of "liberating" the Land of Israel, or Palestine, from Jewish control. The problem with the name was that to liberate means "to free (something, such as a country) from domination by a foreign power," [6] but there never was an officially recognized country called Palestine, so how could they possibly liberate it? They can possibly invade it and steal it from Israel, which, after all, had a long history as a sovereign nation until the Romans conquered and exiled the Jews, but the Arabs cannot liberate it.

The semantic strategy of calling their main

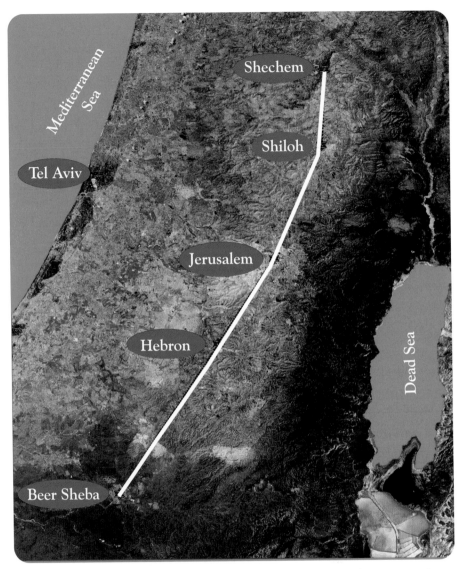

**Not "the West Bank":** The Road of the Patriarchs was and remains the axis of Israel's Biblical cities starting on the mountain ridge of the heartland in Samaria and moving southward into Judea and then the Negev, on the road once traveled by the Biblical leaders of Israel.

organization the "Palestine Liberation Organization" very effectively caused people to think that they once had a country, which they claim was taken from them by the Israelis, when in fact, no such country ever existed!

Nonetheless, the word "Palestine" actually does make sense, since the Hebrew root of the word is "palash," which means "to invade" or "to rob" or "to take something/territory that does not belong to you." [7] Since that is what they are trying to do with their so-called liberation movement, the term Palestine is actually quite appropriate and speaks volumes about their not-so-noble intentions.

The semantic game has continued. During Israel's War of Independence in 1948, the Kingdom of Jordan captured the regions of Judea and Samaria, the central mountainous region, which includes major cities and towns from Israel's history, such as Shiloh, Hebron, Bethlehem, Jericho, and Bethel. In another clever semantic maneuver, the Arabs ignored the historical terms Judea and Samaria and started calling the region the "West Bank." The world willingly adopted the new terminology, and even some Israeli newspapers adopted the geographically and politically inaccurate term, continuing to do so to this day, thus proving to be true the words of Senator Moynihan cited earlier, "It is perfectly predictable that they should misuse words to conceal their real nature. But must we aid them in that effort by repeating those words?"

While the term West Bank is used to subtly hide the historical names Judea and Samaria, calling the areas that Israel recaptured in the Six Day War of 1967 "occupied territories" is a much more explicit and politically obvious strategy. Only the most blatantly anti-

Israel journalists and politicians use that term, because of its more obvious bias.

Then, of course, we have the term "settlements," which refers to the reestablished Jewish communities in Judea and Samaria, and "settlers," which refers to the Jewish residents of those communities. The term "settlers" is defined as "someone who settles in a new region or colony," [8] and is used to ascribe semantic illegitimacy, and therefore, political illegitimacy to those communities and residents. The obvious implication intended is that those Israelis who live in these communities have no historical basis for being there, although the reality is that nothing could be farther from the truth, since Judea and Samaria is the cradle of Jewish civilization, where the Patriarchs and Matriarchs of Israel walked and are now buried, where the Prophets of Israel preached, and where extensive archeology has revealed Biblical accounts as actual history.

The concept of "settler colonialism" has been applied with almost unique vehemence against Israel. But the fact that Jews are the indigenous population of the region can be proven easily, as we have already done through historical facts. In contrast, historical and genealogical evidence shows that the Arabs who call themselves Palestinians descend primarily from three primary groups: Muslim invaders, Arab immigrants, and local converts to Islam. The Muslim conquest of Byzantine Palestine in the 7th century CE is a textbook example of settler-colonialism, as is subsequent immigration, particularly during the 19th and 20th centuries under the Ottoman and British Empires. [9]

The enemy's war of semantics can only be defeated by pointing out falsehood and spreading truth, which brings us to another semantic war – the culture war that is well-underway in America – with a multi-faceted agenda that has been aggressively pursued since the 1960s, although much of the public hasn't noticed the aggressive radical Left agenda that has been transforming America with the help of semantics. Until recently, this strategy has succeeded in remaining mostly under the radar, and therefore, has been extremely efficient in forcing its semantic agenda down an unsuspecting public's throat.

It's important to remember that this entire strategy isn't innocent linguistic drift or slang; it is a conscious effort to reshape society. The schemes include redefining words for personal gain, using modifiers to alter the meaning of a word, replacing technical words with colloquial ones, and creating new words. Each of these is a bullying tactic, which distorts effective discourse.

It starts with misusing words or defining them based on circumstance rather than objective meaning. The entire purpose of defined language is to hold constant meaning so others can understand. Situational use starts to condition how people feel about words, building up a new connotation. [10]

When brainwashing is the goal, distorting connotation is essential, and the Left has turned it into a fine art. We can begin with the word "liberal," which, by definition, refers to one who is open-minded. [11] Because the term has become almost standard, those who do not identify with the Left often find themselves referring to dogmatic leftists as liberals, even though many of them are not open-minded in the least.

A more recent term that has really taken off is "progressive," defined as "one believing in moderate political change and especially social improvement by governmental action." [12] Who could disagree with that? Don't we all like moderation in good measure and moderate action to help society? The problem is that the Left has hijacked the word to mean "a forward-thinking person," and in fact, that is what most people think when they hear the term. However, when we think of the progressive wing of the Democratic Party, we think of Bernie Sanders and Alexandria Ocasio-Cortez (AOC), self-described Socialists, extremists whose ideas are rooted in the now-debunked doctrine of Communism. Furthermore, leftists will rarely use the term "Communist" to describe themselves, nor will they identify themselves publicly as Marxists, but they will identify as Socialist, which has a much more gentle, or "liberal" connotation, if we may use that term in this context.

Another term adopted by the Left, both in America and in Israel, is "social justice." Who could disagree with that? Well, most people would, if it means threats, intimidation, affirmative action (which really means legalized discrimination), dismantling law enforcement, allowing infanticide (abortion at birth), and preventing any mention of God in the schools. That is the agenda of the Left, aided by the semantic deception that is called social justice.

We would be remiss if we ignored the identity politics that have poisoned the Democrats. The semantics have evolved over time, but all with an aggressive ideological agenda. In one of the oldest of the politically loaded distortions, homosexuals must now only be identified as "gays," and don't you dare question whatever happened to "happy," the original meaning of the word, or you will be accused of "homophobia." Furthermore, if you say that God gives life to us as males and females, you might be accused of "transphobia."

In one of the new 2021 proposals heralding the ascendance of the radical Left, but wholly based on gender insanity and an assault on the traditional family, House Speaker Nancy Pelosi (D-CA) proposed forbidding the use of terms, such as "mother, father, daughter, son, brother, or sister" in the House of Representatives. What about the unique embryonic bond between mother and daughter, you ask? No longer important, due to progressive gender changes. If this edict is passed, no longer would it be permitted to use the words "himself" or "herself", which would become "themself", a new nonsensical term that defies grammatical logic. The radical bulls in the china shop are on the warpath, with identity politics run amok. When the totalitarian thought police are doing their vital work, stay out of the way, or you will be censored and you will be called every name in the book, unless those names have by then been removed, as well. [13]

Furthermore, on the topic of make-believe phobias that certainly do not pass any clinical test, if you criticize Muslim fundamentalist extremism, you will be labeled "Islamophobic," another new quasi-psychiatric term. That is to say, that we have nothing to fear from radical Islam and its noble characteristics, such as child abuse, wife-beating, terrorism, and intolerance of those who disagree with you.

When it comes to racial terms, to use the term "colored person" is now considered by political correctness to be racist, presumably because of historical negative connotations or usage, but "person of color" is now the acceptable term all are required to use. "Good Morning

America" co-anchor Amy Robach recently apologized after being harshly criticized for saying "colored people" on a broadcast of the ABC program. It was identified by many as a racial slur, even though it is only a slight shift in the juxtaposition of the words. [14]

Somehow, it is fine nowadays to refer to white people as Caucasians, but if you say Negros, you may be blasted as racist, even though that is a racially accurate term that was used often by black civil rights activists, including Dr. Martin Luther King Jr, during the Civil Rights Movement.

And, of course, only a racist would say that "all lives matter," another "slur" for which many educators and media figures have been rushing to apologize recently.

The excessive emphasis on identity politics and terminology has lost all proportion, as the Left has aggressively pursued a policy of semantic politics on steroids, in order to make conservatives and independents obedient and keep them on the defensive. That strategy is accomplishing its goals in the educational realm, and in the mainstream media, at the very least. The leftist ideologues know well that changing the educational system and the media is what has staying power, and given that reality, the changers of terminology have succeeded beyond their wildest expectations.

Using the example of socialism, once identified with dictators like Lenin, Stalin, Mao, and Castro, the results of decades of brainwashing and semantic gymnastics are seen in American youth. A Gallup poll carried out over ten years has found that since 2010, young adults' positive ratings of socialism have hovered near 50%, while the rate for Gen Xers has been consistently near 34% and near 30% for baby boomers/traditionalists.

At the same time, since 2010, young adults' overall opinion of capitalism has deteriorated to the point that capitalism and socialism are tied in popularity among this age group. This pattern was first observed in 2018 and remains the case today. Perhaps surprisingly to many, in this same study, 83% of young adults still have a positive view of "free enterprise." [15]

This apparent contradiction indicates that the educational system is failing in giving its students an accurate understanding of the terminology. Socialism is certainly not synonymous with a roaring free enterprise economy and the great creativity and human inventiveness that the free market encourages, and which the Founders had envisioned. Socialism is synonymous with overbearing government economic control and, by extension, thought control, very often leading to social engineering and the most brutal suppression of ideas.

*"Don't you see that the whole aim of Newspeak is to narrow the range of thought? In the end we shall make thoughtcrime literally impossible, because there will be no words in which to express it."*

(From George Orwell's "1984") [16]

Orwell's "1984" was written as satire, but with an extremely clear message for our times. Orwell had watched the Bolshevik (Soviet) Revolution in Russia and volunteered to fight against the Fascist government in the Spanish Civil War. At first supportive of the Russian Revolution, he changed his opinions after realizing that behind the veneer of justice and equality lurked widespread famines, forced labor, internal power struggles, and political repression. While fighting in the Spanish Civil War, Orwell became disillusioned with elements within the resistance forces that he felt wanted to replace the Fascist government with an authoritarian regime of its own. These experiences provided the author with much of the rationale for his book.

The Spanish Civil War catalyzed Orwell and made him highly critical of authoritarian tendencies on the Left. In his book, the ruling Party's brutality, paranoia, and betrayals are drawn from the Great Purges of 1936–1938 in the Soviet Union. Over 600,000 people were killed in an official purge of the Communist Party, in an era that also included widespread repression of the public, police surveillance and execution without trial, as well as an atmosphere of fear. [17]

Furthermore, the rise of Hitler and the scapegoating of Jews and other "undesirables" also had a profound effect on Orwell. He realized that mass media was a key factor in Hitler's rise, enabling prominent figures and organizations to shape public opinion on a broad scale. In "1984," the intrusive telescreens and the Party's frequent parades and events are drawn from Nazi Party public propaganda and its marches and rallies. [18]

The thought control that has dominated authoritarian regimes throughout history, and in particular, in the past century, should send chills through the bones of every American. As Orwell has revealed to us all too clearly, thought control begins with the use of language, which is exploited to move public opinion to where the presumptive rulers want it to be. The American Left has learned that lesson well and has been methodically pursuing its goals since the end of the 1960s, when its leadership, in all of its facets, understood that the time for the revolution had not yet come. They then got to work to create the ideological infrastructure that would be the building blocks for what they see as the coming revolution.

Have no illusions – The ideologues of groups like Black Lives Matter, along with the ideological thugs of Antifa, have their eyes on the revolutionary prize, but they understand that it is a process in which sematic manipulation plays a central role. The magnificent American system, which has represented the pinnacle of Judeo-Christian civilization, is under attack today, but the intimidating street mobs are only one, although very noticeable, aspect. It is a multi-pronged attack, not by genuine liberals who want a more inclusive society, but by radicals who want to create a Marxist system in which the identity politics and thought control increasingly promoted by the Democrats and their cohorts in the mainstream media will be front and center.

If that onslaught continues to reap success, it will be such a toxic potion that it will forever transform the United States from a vibrant republic in which inalienable rights are valued and freedoms honored, to a rigid system in which thought control will be implemented, as in Orwell's vision, and Lenin's reality. Social engineering rules, such as the Chinese Communist Party's "One child per family" will be only the tip of the iceberg, as the leftist goon squads that have taken over the streets at will in many Democrat-controlled cities will aggressively enforce a sad caricature of America, the once proud land of the free, that will be unrecognizable.

*Chapter Eight*
# Family, Education, and Hard Work Matter

*"Honor your father and your mother, so that your days will be lengthened upon the land that the Lord your God is giving to you."*

(Exodus 20:12)

*"The richest inheritance any child can have is a stable, loving, disciplined family life."*

(Daniel Patrick Moynihan) [1]

I have been living in Israel for over twenty-eight years, but prior to that, I lived in the United States, where I taught for eight years in New York City public schools before making the big move to Israel. The first school that I taught in was an elementary school in a lower middle-class neighborhood in Brooklyn, which consisted of 90% black students. My philosophy of teaching involved a lot of social interaction between students and a lot of verbal and written discussion about values. One thing that soon became clear was that family, or the lack of traditional family structure that could provide security in their lives, was something that bothered these students terribly. In one of our discussions, it became evident that only seven out of twenty-seven students in this class of fifth graders had fathers who they saw at least once a week.

As part of my simultaneous graduate studies in Education, I decided to explore this further with a small-scale research project called, "Do Boys Need Fathers?"

The professor who advised me how to structure the project and which questions to ask in my interviews with the children was a woman named Lenora Fulani, who, when she wasn't teaching education/psychology courses, was a political leader in the ideologically socialist Independence Party, which at that time had some influence in New York City politics. Anyhow, the unavoidable conclusion from my research was that indeed, boys do need or at least strongly desire the guidance of fathers. Professor Fulani was noticeably displeased with the results and she made that clear to me in her written comments, which apparently were influenced by her extreme Left political views, since as we now know, the radical Left is not very supportive of the ideal of the traditional American family of husband, wife, and children. I was also puzzled by her seeming hostility towards me, which I could not pin down at the time. Much as black people are very sensitive to racism, Jews are very sensitive to possible anti-Semitism, but since I had not yet heard any negative statements from her about Jews or Israel, I pushed those thoughts to the side. However, in 2005, when campaigning Mayor Michael Bloomberg was seeking her endorsement and that of her party, a controversy erupted in which she was forced to defend her 1995 comments as Independence Party leader that "Jews do the dirtiest work of capitalism to function as mass murderers of people of color." Bloomberg subsequently disavowed her support (while continuing to seek that of her party) and Fulani eventually gave a half-baked apology that was not really an apology. [2]

Only much later did I realize that my personal encounter with Fulani was indicative of a certain hostility in the radical Left not just towards Jews and Israel, but also towards the traditional family, which until the 1960s had been one of the pillars of Judeo-Christian civilization. With the left-wing movement's aggressive promotion of LBGTQ as an alternate ideal, the hostility toward the traditional, or nuclear family has only increased. The lesbian founders of BLM made that one of the centerpieces in their radical message.

This from the BLM website:

*"We foster a queer-affirming network. When we gather, we do so with the intention of freeing ourselves from the tight grip of heteronormative thinking..."*

One BLM supporter ominously explained it in such a way that exposed his own confusion:

*"A coalition of queer black feminist Marxists really can't be stopped. The traditional family will crumble into multitudes of communal gender fluid multiracial cooperative coalitions built on dynamic definitions and installations of love."* [3]

And it's not only BLM that vehemently opposes any traditional views of family and gender. The radical MoveOn organization boasts of its "progressive" view of gender, proclaiming that of "the state and local candidates we endorsed, 72% were people of color, 64% **identified** as women." [4]

Apparently, that means that a woman with female genitalia who doesn't **identify** as a woman is not a woman. For the radicals, identity is everything, but only if it fits the radical anti-traditional stereotypes.

In addition to its inability to clearly define its own familial replacement for the nuclear family, the strange romance of the ideological Left with anti-Semitism has only grown over time, as the Left has become more extreme, adopting the social/political philosophy known as Intersectionality. The term is loosely defined as the complex, cumulative way in which the effects of multiple forms of discrimination (such as racism, sexism, and classism) combine, overlap, or intersect, especially in the experiences of marginalized individuals or groups. [5]

Kimberlé Crenshaw, a professor at both Columbia University Law School and the University of California in Los Angeles, is the one who coined the term some thirty years ago. As she explains it, there was no "rational" explanation for the racial wealth gap that existed in 1982 and persists today, or for minority under-representation in spaces that were purportedly based on "colorblind" standards. Rather, as Crenshaw wrote, discrimination remains because of the "stubborn endurance of the structures of white dominance" – in other words, the American legal and socioeconomic order was largely built on racism. [6]

Intersectionality has become the guiding light of the American Left, from Occupy Wall Street to the Women's March to BLM and Antifa. This is the ideological basis for the frequently heard charge of "systemic racism."

The problem is that in a merit-based United States of America, there is no such thing as "minority under-representation." Of course, there are always going to be isolated cases of discrimination based on race, ethnicity, religion, or gender, but there is nothing systemic about it. When everyone has civil rights and discrimination is illegal, people can usually get ahead on merit regardless of ethnicity, but that advancement usually depends on a strong family structure, schooling, a lot of hard work, perseverance, and faith. These factors are several of the very practical solutions that provide a positive response to discrimination, but this social challenge is hardly ever discussed honestly, even though there is no better solution for the lack of advancement than this.

The Jewish experience has a wealth of lessons in the realm of combatting and overcoming discrimination, based on those values, from which Jews have taken potential negatives and turned them into positives.

Just as it was in Biblical times, the traditional family, perhaps more than any single factor has been the bedrock of the Jewish people that has guided this people's morality through the many centuries of dispersion. While so many other ethnic groups that have been afflicted with poverty and discrimination have watched as their family units disintegrated, or perhaps even worse, never came to be, with many thousands of children being born out of wedlock, the Jewish experience was different.

In ancient Egypt, the Israelites were enslaved for hundreds of years, but the family unit remained intact, as did their faith that they would eventually be redeemed. In ancient Israel, as well, the family unit was strong, and although there was some polygamy (as there was in the rest of the world), it was rare, and decreased over time. For at least the past one thousand years, the traditional husband, wife, and children family has been remarkably resilient in Jewish communities around the world. The song of praise to the Jewish wife and mother, known as "Woman of Valor," which is sung to this day in Jewish households around the world every Sabbath evening, has set the family tone for countless generations: [7]

*"She speaks with wisdom, and faithful instruction is on her tongue. She watches over the affairs of her household and does*

*not eat the bread of idleness. Many women do noble things, but you surpass them all."*

(Proverbs 31)

For hundreds of years in eastern Europe, Jews suffered from centuries of poverty and discrimination, Nonetheless, in most cases, the traditional family units remained intact, despite the challenges. Suspicion and hatred of the Jews was by that time widespread, but an event occurred in 1772 that was to leave an indelible mark on the Russian-Jewish relationship. The continuing expansion of the Russian Empire saw the Russian annexation of a substantial portion of Poland. As a result of this first partition of Poland, Russia inherited a Jewish population of 200,000 people. Through the subsequent partitions of 1793 and 1795, which added other Polish-Lithuanian provinces to the empire, the number of Jews grew to 900,000. These partitions presented the Russians with a dilemma. Their historic anti-Semitism prevented them from allowing the Jews to integrate with the Russian population, so various ordinances were enacted to prevent such integration.

The first manifesto issued by the Russian ruler Catherine the Great to the new provinces under her control was clearly indicative of the discriminatory policy to be followed under Tsarist rule. The proclamation, which was dated August 16, 1772, stated that the locale in which the Jews could exercise the rights enjoyed under their previous government was to be specifically limited to the territory in which they were living at the time of the partition. No such restriction was placed on other new inhabitants of the empire.

In 1791, a decree was issued, specifically barring the

Jews from definite areas. April of 1835 saw the passage of legislation by the government of Nicholas I which clearly defined the boundaries of what was called the Pale of Settlement, limiting the Jews to specific towns and regions. Opportunities in schooling and work were also strictly limited. [8]

Despite all of those barriers to advancement, the religious Jewish family was the norm, as was the traditional intact Jewish family, divorce was rare, and a child born out of wedlock in the Pale of Settlement was virtually unheard of. The mother has always been the anchor of the traditional Jewish family, but fathers have always been responsible for the children's Torah education, and therefore, have usually been very involved, as well.

The initial immigration of Jews to the United States en masse was in the mid-19th century, when some 200,000 Jews immigrated to the US, mostly from Germany and central Europe. Most of them were Reform Jews, well-established, who saw themselves as Germans and Americans more than as Jews. They scattered across the continent and set up businesses, from small stores and factories to companies that eventually became financial giants like Lehman Brothers and Goldman Sachs.

Discrimination was later encountered by the next, much larger wave of Jewish immigrants who moved to America to escape discrimination and horrible persecution in Europe and elsewhere. The great wave of immigration began in 1882. These new arrivals were poor and also more visibly and unashamedly Jewish, both in appearance and comportment, and the discrimination they encountered created seemingly insurmountable challenges. But for the Jews, this was nothing new.

The immigrants reached America on crowded boats,

**No Honest Job was Demeaning:** Jews hard at work in a makeshift garment workshop in New York. While there was discrimination, education and hard work were always the Jewish standard for success in the free market. No excuses, no identity politics, no days of rage.

and as noted, most of them were very poor. Most of them lived in crowded and filthy slums in New York, mostly in Brooklyn and the Lower East Side (of Manhattan), though some eventually moved on to other cities, like Philadelphia, Boston, and Chicago. Dr. Robert Rockaway, who studied that period, wrote that 80% of US Jews were employed in manual work before World War I, most of them in textile factories. Many workplaces were blocked to the Jews due to an anti-Semitic campaign led by industrialist Henry Ford.

The Jewish immigrants, however, emerged from poverty and made faster progress than any other group of immigrants. Anti-Semitism weakened after World War II and the restrictions on hiring Jews were reduced and later canceled as part of the 1964 Civil Rights Act.

As they moved out of poverty, Jews integrated into society. They moved from the slums to the suburbs, abandoned the Yiddish language and adopted the clothes, culture, slang, dating and shopping habits of the non-Jewish elite. [9]

Alongside the Jews, millions of immigrants arrived in the US from Ireland, Italy, China, and dozens of other countries. They, too, have achieved a lot and have settled down since then, but research indicates that the Jews have succeeded more than everyone, and much of the credit goes to Jewish education. For example, the Jewish-American student organization Hillel found that 9 to 33% of students in leading universities in the US are Jewish. This, despite the fact that the Jewish population in the United States rarely surpassed 3% of the overall population. [10]

It should be pointed out that the Jewish emphasis on study came from the Jewish faith tradition of comprehensive Torah learning that has continued to this day, mostly among the Orthodox, the more fervently religious. Until a couple of generations ago, virtually all Jews were in that tradition. The value of intense learning has been passed on from generation to generation and is deeply engrained in the Jewish culture.

*"And teach them to your children, speak of it to them when you are sitting at home, when you are walking on the way, when you lie down and when you rise up."*

(Deuteronomy 11:19)

**The Sanctity of Study:** The strong Jewish emphasis on education is rooted in the tradition of intensive Torah study, as seen here in a small Jerusalem study hall.

Therefore, it is important to understand that there was never affirmative action for Jews, nor was it ever desired. The message from parents to children was always, "Work hard and you will achieve!"

"The Jewish tradition always sanctified studying, and the Jews made an effort to study from the moment they arrived in America," says Danny Halperin, Israel's former economic attaché in Washington. "In addition, the Jews have a strong tradition of business entrepreneurship. They progressed because many areas were blocked to them. Many Irish were integrated into the police force, for example, but very few Jews. The Jews entered and even created new fields in which there was a need for people with initiative. For example, they were not integrated into traditional banking field, so they established the investment banking." [11]

In other words, American Jews did not succeed **despite the fact** that there was discrimination against them, but paradoxically, their values of hard work, education, perseverance, and positive thinking were actually activated and enhanced **because** there was discrimination against them. They knew that they needed to work harder and think creatively to get ahead, which only made them work harder. Complaining about discrimination and having "days of rage" in order to riot and loot stores was absolutely not the Jewish way – overcoming obstacles through hard work and creativity was. In fact, the rise of the tiny, modern State of Israel as a technological and military power and a bastion of freedom in a vast sea of oppressive Islamic countries is a result of that enterprising hard-working positive spirit.

"The Jews had to excel in order to survive," says Avia Spivak, a professor of economics and former Bank of Israel deputy governor. "I once had a student of Russian descent, who told me that his parents said to him, 'You must be the best, because then you might get a small role.' That was the situation of the Jews abroad, and in America, too, until the 1960s. The most prestigious universities did not take in Jewish students, so they studied in (less prestigious) colleges and got the best grades. When the discrimination disappeared, the Jews reached the top ... I think Jews succeeded in America in particular because capitalism is good for the Jews. Jews have a tendency for entrepreneurship, they study more and have quick perception, know how to seize opportunities, and have networking skills. A competitive environment gives Jews an advantage." [12]

While some would argue that intersectionality accurately describes that systemic racism still exists, it is fatally flawed in its lack of emphasis on positive solutions. Anyone who is obsessed with blaming others rather than adopting self-reflection, followed by hard work, will not get ahead. The Jews have been enslaved, assaulted, discriminated against, and slaughtered by the millions, but have always triumphed through the values described above.

In a recent article, Rabbi Emanuel Feldman delivers a (slightly paraphrased) mini sermon of tough love that he would like black pastors to share with parents of black children. His words may sound harsh to some, but they are worth listening to:

*"As your spiritual leader, I say to you, Restore the Bible into your children's lives. Teach them that there is a God, teach them the Ten Commandments, to honor their parents; teach them thou shalt not steal, thou shalt not murder, thou shalt not commit adultery. Teach them that not every wish and desire needs to be satisfied immediately; teach them the joys of occasional self-denial.*

*"The black future is being destroyed by thuggery and criminal behavior. When your pickup trucks back up to department stores into which you have broken, and you load up with everything you can put your hands on – is this the kind of behavior that creates a future for blacks? Yes, I know the resentments, the biases, the wounds, but this is not the way to fight them.*

*"What you are doing is confirming the worst prejudices about us. Whites say that blacks have a high criminal rate. How do we react? By breaking into stores. Whites say we have no respect for authority. How do we react? By burning down police stations.*

*"I know my words are not politically correct, and I assume I will be roundly calumniated if not worse after this sermon, but I care too much about my black people to remain silent. What I say today is obvious, but they are not being uttered – in churches, in newspapers, nor in any media. The truth must be spoken. If you really believe that black lives matter now and tomorrow, you will take to heart my words this day."*[13]

While the Jews have accomplished more than most based on the value system of education, hard work, perseverance, and faith, many others of different races and religions have, as well. And even though the traditional father and mother family is the ideal, there are many who don't have it, but still have achieved a lot, due to the impact of one dominant parent or parental figure who succeeded in instilling those strong values. While we can point to many good examples, a couple of notable black Americans will suffice. They are both famous and are from opposite ends of the political spectrum, but that's not at all relevant to the principles that we have been emphasizing. In fact, it proves that this is not about politics. It is all about the time-proven values that many on the Left want to do away with, or, even worse, to denounce as racist.

Renowned neurosurgeon, presidential candidate, and Housing and Urban Development Secretary in the Trump administration since 2017, Dr. Ben Carson, who happens to be black, has often shared his personal story, which was made into a popular movie, *Gifted Hands: The Ben Carson Story*. It is, indeed, a story of emphasis on education, on hard work, and on faith, all of which helped him to achieve tremendously in life. Carson has praised his mother, who was divorced and who cleaned homes for a living. Mrs. Carson did not waste her time

**Hard Work Breeds Success:** For Dr. Ben Carson, renowned surgeon, presidential candidate, and Housing and Urban Development Secretary in the Trump administration, success was a product of his enormous efforts, humility, faith – and a mother who pushed those values.

complaining about "white privilege" and discrimination that forced her into a low-paying job. The only "forcing" that was discussed in the Carson home was when she forced her children to turn off the television and to read in order to learn. Those were lessons well learned and never forgotten. Carson became the Director of Pediatric Neurosurgery at the Johns Hopkins Children's Center in 1984 at age 33; he was the youngest chief of pediatric neurosurgery in the United States. Carson has received numerous honors for his neurosurgery work, including more than 60 honorary doctorate degrees and numerous national merit citations. Carson's achievements include performing the only successful separation of conjoined twins joined at the back of the head; performing the first successful neurosurgical procedure on a fetus inside the womb; performing the first completely successful separation of type-2 vertical craniopagus twins; developing new methods to treat brain-stem tumors; and revitalizing hemispherectomy techniques for controlling seizures. He wrote over 100 neurosurgical publications. He retired from medicine in 2013, before entering the world of politics, leading to his current position in the Trump Cabinet. Hard work, perseverance, and faith got Ben Carson to where he is today. [14]

**The Will to Succeed:** Despite tough times in a difficult childhood, Oprah Winfrey was a hard-working student who had the drive to succeed and a grandmother who taught her to believe in herself. Despite early instability in her life, she entered adulthood believing that no obstacle was too great to overcome with great effort.

Oprah Winfrey was born into a poor Mississippi family in 1954, but that did not stop her from achieving unparalleled success through a lot of hard work and perseverance. After Winfrey's birth, her mother traveled north, and Winfrey spent her first six years living in rural poverty with her maternal grandmother. Her grandmother was so poor that Winfrey often wore dresses made of potato sacks, for which other children made fun of her. Her grandmother taught her to read before the age of three and took her to the local church, where she was nicknamed "The Preacher" for her ability to recite Bible verses, which perhaps gave her a love for learning. While that was very positive, her childhood was otherwise very unstable, and she was bounced from place to place. After she was abused and molested by two family members and a family friend, she ran away from home at the age of thirteen. At fourteen, she had a child out of wedlock – the child died shortly after.

Despite that adversity, Winfrey was already an intelligent and driven young woman who took her studies very seriously, and she was awarded a scholarship to Tennessee State University. Following an appearance in a local beauty pageant, she went on to become the first African American TV correspondent in the state at the young age of nineteen. She later moved to Chicago, where she began work on her very own morning show. It would later be widely known as "The Oprah Winfrey Show." She was the first woman in history to own and produce her own talk show. The popular show aired for 25 seasons, from 1986 to 2011. Since moving on from her talk show, Winfrey founded OWN, the Oprah Winfrey Network. [15]

Carson and Winfrey both have achieved great stardom, but obviously there are many lesser knowns who have also achieved a lot in their own fields of endeavor. Furthermore, these two stellar role models both managed to achieve without the benefit of an intact family, although both would certainly have preferred a loving and present mother and father as the ideal situation. However, in each of their cases, there was a family member who strongly emphasized the values of hard work, education, perseverance, and faith which they absorbed, and those values carried them to great heights.

The message to be learned is this: What does **not** help individuals who face discrimination to advance in this world is negativity, blaming others, and demanding hand-outs, otherwise known as "free stuff." What **does** help is a system of sound values, usually acquired through a supportive family that encourages learning, a strong emphasis on education, and a tremendous amount of hard work and perseverance. All of these matter, and in a big way. Creativity and initiative can be added into the mix, and, as we've noted, a lot of faith in God certainly helps, as well.

Despite the positive example provided by the Jewish experience in overcoming adversity through hard work, the leftist bias persists against Jews and Israel, with a particular hatred expressed towards Zionism, the liberation movement of the Jewish people. The disturbing anti-Semitism experienced by the far too many American Jews involved with the various "resistance" groups should be seen for what it is, not denied and not ignored. There are many Jews who are disconnected from their Jewish heritage, from their Biblical roots, and from the Land of Israel and for that reason, many of them involve themselves with the left-wing organizations that bash Zionism, not understanding that negating the one Jewish state is the same as negating the Jews.

For those who say that those on the Left cannot be anti-Semitic or racist, BLM, for example, has been guided to anti-Semitism by its concept of "intersectionality," which, as we discussed earlier, argues that all oppressions are interlinked and cannot be solved alone. Somehow from this they conclude, with not a shred of evidence, and it has been clearly stated in the BLM platform, that Israel is carrying out "genocide" against the Palestinians. BLM activists have visited Gaza and expressed a sympathetic attitude towards terrorist groups like Hamas, which does call for the genocide of Jews and actively engages in some of the most brutal forms of terrorism, including bus bombings, shootings, stabbings, and rock-throwing ambushes. [16]

Several years ago, a group of BLM activists from Chicago, visiting Israel on a fact-finding tour, were convinced by their guide to visit Shiloh in Samaria. The stated purpose of the morning visit was to see the projects of Shiloh Israel Children's Fund, which I had founded some years prior, after my then three-year-old son and I were shot and wounded in a terror attack.

We visited our main therapeutic-educational campus, where so many Israeli children, victims of radical Muslim terrorism, have been treated for trauma. Despite receiving what is for most visitors a moving, informative learning experience about the painful challenges faced by the residents of the Biblical heartland communities, the BLM visitors spent much of their time complaining about the "crimes" and the "genocide" that they claimed Israel is guilty of. Their ignorance of the facts was so appalling that one of the gentle, sensitive therapists who had heard everything was in shock and couldn't understand where the blind hatred was coming from, until I explained to her what the BLM platform says about Israel.

Fortunately, there have been some great leaders who have been able to see through the facade of anti-racism presented by those who are actually bigots themselves:

On October 27, 1967, just a few months after the Six Day War, in which Israel, under attack from all sides, had recaptured Jerusalem, Judea, Samaria and the Golan Heights, in addition to other territories, Dr. Martin Luther King Jr. had dinner with a group of students from Harvard University in Boston. Professor Seymour Martin Lipset was present and recalls how one of the students criticized Zionists. Dr. King was incensed, saying "Don't talk like that!" – and continued:

*"When people criticize Zionists, they mean Jews. You're talking anti-Semitism!"*[17]

The concept of intersectionality misses the boat by choosing which liberation movements fit its narrative of leftist or radical Muslim revolution, often choosing the liberation movements that do not deserve support (certainly not the Zionists/Jews) and then ascribing blame on white people and some people who are not so white, making unreasonable and often racist demands, and backing those demands with either the threat of violence and chaos, or actual violence and chaos.

A bold strategy of encouraging the traditional family, a passion for education, and a lot of hard work and perseverance would do wonders for reversing the suffering of many black communities in America. Unfortunately, the BLM radicals have preferred to play a historically inaccurate blame game. Such a strategy makes no sense, if the real goal is to give people skills and knowledge that can bring them out of poverty and into advancement on their own merit.

The BLM model is, however, an appropriate strategy, if their actual intent is to create internal social warfare, bedlam, and racial strife. Sadly, that is the approach that most of the radical groups have adopted.

## Chapter Nine
# Did Israeli Socialism Work?

*"The inherent vice of capitalism is the unequal sharing of blessings; the inherent virtue of socialism is the equal sharing of miseries."*

(Winston Churchill) [1]

*"The problem with socialism is that you eventually run out of other peoples' money."*

(Margaret Thatcher) [2]

*"A socialist is someone who has read Lenin and Marx. An anti-socialist is someone who understands Lenin and Marx."*

(Ronald Reagan) [3]

T he ideology of socialism, which recently has become all the rage among young Americans, is actually a mere one hundred years old, but with a history that we should be able to learn from. The socialist or communist system has been tried in many important countries, including the former Soviet Union and its satellites, as well as China, Vietnam, North Korea, and Cuba. Since 1918, socialism has been tried in 64 countries and has consistently failed, but the recent Marxist movements have been driven by the new-found American passion for socialism. According to the most recent Gallup poll, 57% of Democrats now view socialism favorably, while only 47% view capitalism favorably. [4]

Since we are still trying to learn what we can from the Jewish experience, and specifically from Israel, where do

**Communist/Socialist Unity:** Legendary Socialist leaders like Cuba's Fidel Castro and Hugo Chavez of Venezuela destroyed free market economies and brought the people to their knees by nationalizing industry, suppressing the press, suppressing speech, manipulating electoral laws, and massive arresting and exiling of government critics.

the Jews stand on all of this socialism stuff? Isn't it true that American Jews (with the notable recent exception of the relatively small, but steadily growing Orthodox Jewish population) have historically, on average, supported the Democrats in much larger numbers, and have been connected to left-wing movements?

Let me preface my response by stating that the answer is actually quite complicated. Jews, who have always been typified by their search for truth, have been both among the greatest proponents, and the most vociferous opponents, of socialism.

Before we go on, let's first deal with the elephant in the room. It is a fact that two of the great minds of Marxism were Jews, specifically its creator Karl Marx, who was a lapsed Russian Jew who had no Jewish content in his life other than the desire to search for what he considered as truth.

In the mid-20th century, socialist theorist Saul Alinsky was a Jewishly-disconnected American Jew, whose main religious passion was "community-organizing" as a means of advancing the socialist agenda. Alinsky's highly influential book, "Rules for Radicals: A Pragmatic Primer for Realistic Radicals", guided the post 1960's generation of establishment radicals, such as the former community organizer from Chicago, Barack Obama and his colleague Hillary Clinton, who chose Alinsky as the topic for her doctoral dissertation.

More recently, there have been many Jews who have been active in support of the America-hating Marxist movements, most notably another well-known JINO (Jew in name only), billionaire George Soros, [5] who has given many millions to the Marxist movements and has also been known to give substantial financial support to avowedly anti-Israel organizations, including those that promote and support BDS, the movement to boycott Israel and to punish those that do business with Israel. [6]

Much of Soros's focus has been directed towards funding the campaigns of left-wing extremists in district attorney races in cities like Philadelphia, St. Louis, Chicago, Boston, and Los Angeles. Traditionally, a prosecutor's job is to enforce the law, but Soros has spent huge sums (some two million dollars just in Los Angeles) to elect radical left-wing ideologues who would instead let murderers and rapists go free while creating havoc in American society. By doing so, he devastates the poor, minority communities that he ostensibly wants to help. [7]

In short, despite Soros's Jewish lineage, he has proven himself, through his massive financial support to such nefarious goals, to be a dangerous enemy of both America and Israel. Many misguided liberals have defended Soros from criticism by invoking the charge of anti-Semitism. We should be very clear that anyone who does so, is thereby slandering the millions of Jews who have suffered from actual anti-Semitism, which sadly, is greatly encouraged by some of the radical leftist organizations that Soros supports with his vast wealth.

However, there are and have been far greater numbers of successful Jewish capitalists in America, and many of them have been specifically targeted by the left-wing movements for their "Wall Street connections." While the "charges" are repugnant, especially since there is nothing wrong with investing in the free market, it is also nothing new, as the Jew-haters at both extremes have always been active in spreading their venom. The difference in our times is that the left-wing anti-Semites have clearly gained prominence. They are much more active, much more vocal, and, apparently, much more numerous, with an additional boost of cooperation from some of their radical Muslim allies, whose efforts at stifling freedom of speech are often expressed in violent shutdown demonstrations when conservative or pro-Israel speakers are scheduled to appear at American colleges.

Jewish socialists aside, it is easy to compile a long list of American Jews who have been, and continue to be, amongst the greatest achievers and job creators in the capitalist system that the Marxists love to hate. Just focusing on the great American department stores and clothing chains in the past century, we see that most were founded by Jewish entrepreneurs, indeed, visionaries, including Macy's, Bergdorf Goodman, Gimbels, Filene's, I Magnin, Neiman-Marcus, Bloomingdales, Rich's of Atlanta, Kauffman's of Pittsburgh, Lazarus of Columbus, Florsheim, Syms, The Gap, Reebok, Timberland, Calvin Klein, Ralph Lauren, and Levi Strauss. If we extend this abbreviated list into the field of cosmetics, we have to include Revlon, Faberge, Estee Lauder, Clairol, Max Factor, Helena Rubinstein, Charles Revson, and others. [8]

In the food service industry, many household name businesses were founded by Jewish entrepreneurs. These have included Dunkin Donuts, Baskin Robbins, Ben & Jerry's, Haagen Dazs, Snapple, and Starbucks. To list all of the Jewish-founded high-tech companies could require another book, but we will suffice with just mentioning Google, Facebook, and Dell. [9]

All of the companies listed above were founded by great entrepreneurs, capitalists, and free market advocates. In a Marxist system, the creative energies that produced these great companies would not have been able to flourish. Yes, Jews have historically been involved in commerce and finance in many other countries when they have been allowed to be involved, both in parts of eastern Europe and in the Arab countries, but it is in America where Jews have thrived enormously by competing in the greatest free enterprise system in the world.

As we discussed earlier, most Jews came to the United States in poverty, with no money to invest and the added obstacle of discrimination against them. Many of the Jewish immigrants started working in the sweatshops of the garment industry in the Lower East

Side of New York City, but before long, and mostly due to a lot of hard work, long hours, and education, they lifted themselves up from poverty, soon becoming salesmen, managers, retailers, and eventually, many became teachers, doctors, nurses, and lawyers, once the eased up and they were allowed to study professions. As noted earlier, American Jews thrived in the competition of the free market, capitalist system.

Therefore, it may seem ironic that the modern State of Israel was established in 1948 by Jewish socialists, who had fled the former Soviet Union and other European countries that had fallen under its oppressive totalitarian rule.

I recall my first contact with Israeli socialism, if only by remote, when I was still living in Brooklyn in the early 1980s. It was through a conversation with my very first Hebrew teacher, a temporarily transplanted Israeli woman who was living in Manhattan. I recall being puzzled when, with a sigh, she stated, with no particular sense of pride, that "Israel is a very poor country with 'rich' people."

It took some explanation for me to understand what she meant; that the Israel government would routinely put the country into serious debt to subsidize basic needs, as well as some appliances, so that everyone would feel that they had "the good life." The reality, however, was quite different. Salaries in Israel were about a third of comparable salaries in the United States, but most living expenses were the same or higher. Almost everyone in Israel made it through the month with serious overdraft in their bank accounts and would often take out loans from those same banks to temporarily cover the overdraft, thus compounding the recurring financial dilemma.

The socialist Zionist leaders, most having been

influenced by the Soviet Bolshevik system, had effectively established a highly centralized economic system dominated by political cronyism. While the policy of tight government control of the economy as carried out by successive Labor governments failed to create a socialist paradise, they did succeed in building monolithic, unresponsive bureaucratic institutions that held back the country's economic growth for decades. There was also quite a bit of cronyism. If you weren't a member of the Labor party or any of its components, you were reducing your chances of economic survival, since they controlled the Histadrut, the huge labor union, which was a political power, in and of itself. There was also totally nationalized medical insurance, which was represented by a monstrous bureaucracy of a monopoly health fund. The system didn't work at all, with people often waiting many months for essential operations.

Few people were actually happy with the system, but being a resilient people that has lived through far worse challenges, Israelis learned to live in a perpetual state of actual impoverishment, even if the safety net was, at least in theory, widely spread. [10]

It has been said by some that Israeli socialism was successful – for a short while. The original settlers, according to Israeli professor Avi Kay, "sought to create an economy in which market forces were controlled for the benefit of the whole society." Driven by a desire to leave behind their history as victims of penury and prejudice, they sought an egalitarian, labor-oriented socialist society. The initial, (roughly) homogeneous population of less than 1 million drew up centralized plans to convert the desert into green pastures and build efficient state-run companies.

Most early settlers, American Enterprise Institute scholar Joseph Light pointed out, worked either on collective farms called kibbutzim or in state-guaranteed jobs. The kibbutzim were small farming communities in which people did chores in exchange for food and money to live on and pay their bills. There was no private property, people ate in common dining halls, and, in many cases, children under eighteen lived together and not with their parents. Any money earned on the outside was given to the kibbutz. [11]

As noted, a key player in the socialization of Israel was the Histadrut, the General Federation of Labor, subscribers to the socialist dogma that capital exploits labor and that the only way to prevent such "robbery" is to grant control of the means of production to the state. As it proceeded to unionize almost all workers, the Histadrut gained control of nearly every economic and social sector, including the kibbutzim, housing, transportation, banks, social welfare, health care, and education. The federation's political instrument was the Labor party, which effectively ruled Israel from the founding of Israel in 1948 until 1973 and the Yom Kippur War. In the early years, while Israel was struggling valiantly to quickly absorb hundreds of thousands of new immigrants, to take care of housing needs and to rapidly build schools for its burgeoning population, few asked whether any limits should be placed on the role of government. [12]

Despite the need for a grossly oversized military budget to defend this tiny country, which before the 1967 Six Day War was about the size of Delaware and surrounded on all sides by bitter enemies with 700 times Israel's land mass, the Israeli economy seemed to be surviving and even at times thriving, on the surface at least. Real GDP growth from 1955 to 1975 was an astounding 12.6%, putting Israel among the fastest-growing economies in the world, with one of the lowest income differentials. However, this rapid growth was accompanied by rising levels of private consumption and, over time, increasing income inequality. There was an increasing demand for economic reform to free the economy from the government's centralized decision-making. In 1961, supporters of economic liberalization formed the Liberal party – the first political movement committed to a market economy, as Israelis slowly began to question the prevailing socialist system.

The Israeli "economic miracle," which was really a desert mirage, evaporated in 1965 when the country suffered its first major recession. Economic growth halted, and unemployment rose threefold from 1965 to 1967. Before the government could attempt corrective action, the Six Day War erupted, altering Israel's economic and political map. Paradoxically, the war brought short-lived prosperity to Israel, owing to increased military spending and a major influx of workers from the repossession of old/new territories. However, government-led economic growth was accompanied by rapidly accelerating inflation, reaching an annual rate of 17% from 1971 to 1973.

For the first time, there was a serious public debate between supporters of free-enterprise economics and supporters of the traditional socialist arrangements that had ruled the country absolutely since its founding in 1948.

Leading the way for the free market was the future

Nobel Prize winner Milton Friedman, who urged Israeli policymakers to "set your people free" and liberalize the economy. The 1973 war and its economic impacts reinforced the increasing feelings among many Israelis that the Labor party's socialist model could not handle the country's growing economic challenges. This led to the democratic overthrow of the left-wing elites and the end of their unquestioned socialist rule. The 1977 elections resulted in a rousing victory for Menachem Begin's Likud party, with its staunch pro-free-market philosophy. The Likud took as one of its major coalition partners the Liberal party, which we may recall, advocated free enterprise.

Because socialism's roots in Israel were so deep, real reform proceeded slowly and change did not come without great pain. Prime Minister Begin asked Friedman to draw up an ambitious program that would move Israel from socialism toward a free-market economy. His major reforms included fewer government programs and reduced government spending; less government intervention in fiscal, trade, and labor policies; income-tax cuts; and privatization. A great debate ensued between government officials seeking reform and the many special interests that preferred the status quo, primary among them the powerful Histadrut Federation, which frequently closed down the country at will with massive strikes that literally crippled the economy and, at least temporarily, prevented the transformation to the capitalist economy that Begin so strongly advocated. Survival became the name of the game, as the socialist machine was proving to be too entrenched to dismantle, despite Begin's noble goal of a free-market economy.

Meanwhile, the government kept borrowing and

spending and driving up inflation, which averaged 77% for 1978-79 and reached a shocking peak of 450% in 1984-85. The government's share of the economy grew to 76%, while fiscal deficits and national debt skyrocketed. The government printed money through loans from the Bank of Israel, which contributed to the inflation by churning out money.

Finally, in January 1983, the bubble burst, and thousands of private citizens and businesses as well as government-run enterprises faced bankruptcy. Israel was close to collapse. At this critical moment, a sympathetic US president, Ronald Reagan, and his secretary of state, George Shultz, came to the rescue. They offered a grant of $1.5 billion if the Israeli government would agree to abandon its socialist rulebook and adopt a strict program of US-style capitalism, using American-trained professionals. [13]

The Histadrut Labor Federation strongly resisted, unwilling to give up their decades-old power and to concede that socialism was responsible for Israel's economic troubles. However, the people had had enough of soaring inflation and non-existent growth and rejected the Histadrut's policy of resistance. Still, the Israeli government hesitated, unwilling to spend political capital on economic reform. An exasperated Secretary Schulz informed Israel that if it did not begin freeing up the economy, the US would freeze "all monetary transfers" to the country. The threat worked. The Israeli government officially adopted most of the free market "recommendations." [14]

Usually threats of that kind have not worked with Israel, especially when the threats were blatantly political and were against Israel's existential interests

**Reagan and Begin - Two Principled Conservatives:** US President Ronald Reagan and Israeli Prime Minister Menachem Begin were both passionate conservatives who were not afraid to speak their minds. Begin did not happily receive threats, as was the case in his famous Congressional encounter with then Senator Joe Biden (see below), but when President Reagan threatened Israel in order to transform its economy to encourage free market capitalism, Begin happily "gave in" to those demands.

and historical precedent. On June 22, 1982, Prime Minister Begin spoke before the Senate Foreign Relations Committee at the height of the Lebanon War. At that meeting, then Senator Joe Biden attacked Israeli settlements in Judea and Samaria and threatened Begin that if Israel did not immediately cease this activity, the US would cut economic aid to Israel, triggering a fierce response from Begin:

*"Don't threaten us with cutting off your aid. It will not work. I am not a Jew with trembling knees. I am a proud Jew with 3,700 years of civilized history. Nobody came to our aid*

*when we were dying in the gas chambers and ovens. Nobody came to our aid when we were striving to create our country. We paid for it. We fought for it. We died for it. We will stand by our principles. We will defend them. And, when necessary, we will die for them again, with or without your aid ... Do you think that because the US lends us money it is entitled to impose on us what we must do? We are grateful for the assistance we have received, but we are not to be threatened. I am a proud Jew. Three thousand years of culture are behind me, and you will not frighten me with threats. Take note: we do not want a single soldier of yours to die for us."*

Senator Biden was stunned by Begin's emotional response, but the prime minister was speaking from the heart. Biden was threatening Israel's very survival and its most vital and sacred places in its historical homeland. Menachem Begin was a battle-scarred Zionist who would choose his words carefully, but he knew when to take a stand. In this particular case, he did so with a clear demonstration of Jewish pride that Biden was certainly not expecting, but apparently needed to hear. [15]

The difference in the case of the Reagan-Schultz threat was that whether or not it was planned in advance with Begin's knowledge, it was mutually understood to be for Israel's own good. The threat from the US gave Begin the backing to stand against the powerful socialist forces within his country that had kept Israel in a stranglehold for several decades. The opportunity was there to finally free up the economy with the help of a friendly administration and Begin seized the moment.

The impact of the basic shift in Israeli economic policy was immediate and pervasive. Within a year, inflation tumbled from 450% to just 20%, a budget deficit of 15% of GDP shrank to zero, the Histadrut's economic and business empire disappeared along with its political domination, and the Israeli economy was opened up to a sharp increase in imports. Of particular importance was the Israeli high-tech revolution, which led to a 600% increase in investment in Israel, transforming the country into a major player in an increasingly high-tech world. [16]

Today, the State of Israel is known for its innovation and entrepreneurship. In the world of technology, Israel is king. The country has more high-tech start-ups per capita than anywhere else in the world and is second only to the US in venture capital funds. This is an impressive feat for any country, but especially one that is only seventy-three years old and home to just nine million people. Despite its relatively small population, this tiny nation has produced hundreds of tech developments, from everyday items like USB drives to futuristic medical devices that can offer diagnoses in an instant. [17]

Israel has the 3rd most companies listed on the NASDAQ; a remarkable feat given the small size of its economy. Its exports are dominated by the high-tech industry, with approximately half coming from that sector. [18]

Even the kibbutz, that unique model of socialist ideology, which had become almost a symbol of the rise of the State of Israel, has transformed itself by necessity. The kibbutz had become a failed egalitarian, centralized social experiment. Recognizing that fact, it has opened itself up to human creativity and developed into its own unique model of socially sensitive capitalism, which now recognizes that human initiative and freedom are not evil.

In today's kibbutz, most of the children live with their parents and much of the property has become privatized.

Many kibbutzim not only have thriving businesses – including in the tourism industry – that operate exactly like other private enterprises, but some have even decided to embrace the capital market: Twenty-two kibbutz companies are currently listed on stock exchanges in Tel Aviv, New York and London. With annual sales worth $10 billion, the kibbutz companies account for about 10% of Israel's industrial production.

Farming is still important to most kibbutzim, though much less so than during the early years. Indeed, the shift to industry that started in the 1960s and 1970s was an important factor in persuading the kibbutzim to change their ways: they realized that a factory, unlike a farm, is hard to run along egalitarian lines. Someone, in short, had to manage, and someone had to stand at the assembly line, but the transformation of the kibbutz from socialist bastion to capitalist co-operative is, above all, a reflection of the much broader shift in Israeli society. [19]

It is now clear to all that Israel, which just several decades ago was a tiny country under assault from all sides, with a stagnant, socialist economy, has advanced enormously and truly joined the free world in every sense of the word. For this resilient, creative people that has always found ways to survive in the midst of adversity, socialism was never a good match, stifling creativity and private initiative. Israel today is still a tiny country, but its citizens' creativity has burst forth and flourished, due mainly to the removal of red tape, oppressive taxes, and governmental control over people's lives. It can be said today that Israel has a roaring free market economy that has left socialism in the dust. The proof is in the politics. The Labor Party, which totally ruled Israel for its first three decades of existence, controlling all of the institutions of government and patronage, has seen its power dwindled with each succeeding election. There was a momentary resurgence in the 1992 election, but it was too late to turn back the apple cart. The undoing of the socialist economy was too popular to be reversed. In the latest electoral polls taken before Israel's March 2021 elections, it was predicted that the once proudly socialist Labor Party would not even get enough votes to enter the Knesset (Israel's Parliament). Truly, the people have spoken.

One important result of Israel's emergence as a high-tech power, as well as its new status as an energy-exporting nation, is the recent interest by nations in the Arab world to normalize relations with Israel, something that would have been unthinkable just ten years ago. Israel's military capability, combined with its technological know-how, has caused previously hostile nations like the United Arab Emirates, Bahrain, Sudan, and Morocco to seek friendship with the Jewish state. President Trump played a pivotal role in encouraging those developments, especially since he, as a successful businessman, understood the power of self-interest and free markets in bringing people together, but it must be emphasized – the technological advancement and energy independence that Israel is now benefitting from would not have happened without the opening up of the Israeli economy.

The lessons for America are clear. The "power to the people" slogan that became popular during the 1960s when the roots of the current Marxist movements were seeded, referred to the rebellion of the Left against the American established system. However, true power to the people means enabling power to the citizens. Free enterprise gives them that power. It unleashes

**An Economic and Strategic Peace Process:** Israeli Prime Minister Benjamin Netanyahu and US President Donald Trump, with foreign ministers of Bahrain and United Arab Emirates signing the Abraham Accords at the White House in September 2020. Israel's growth as an economic power is one key factor encouraging the Arab interest in normalizing ties with the Jewish state.

the creative, enterprising, hard-working spirit that has made the United States a world leader and the greatest economic force in modern times. Undoing that system by establishing socialist rule would create a rigid government-controlled system that would cease to function on the level that it has until now. The empty shelves in the supermarkets of what was then the communist Soviet Union would only be the tip of the iceberg. If history is any indication of things to come, the harsh restrictions on individual freedom that Vladimir Lenin, Joseph Stalin, Fidel Castro, and Mao Zedong imposed on their citizens would likely follow.

Thousands of young, naive Americans are obediently voting for socialists, but is that what they really want? Do they even know what it means and what it can lead to?

**One Child Good, Two Child Bad:** The two photos below demonstrate the Chinese Communist Party (CCP) attempts to suppress reproductive freedom, and not just through "One Child Better" billboards. The upper photo shows the city of Shuangwang in southern China's Guangxi region in May 25, 2007. Residents of this riot-hit area of southern China demanded that authorities make amends for a brutal three-month campaign to enforce family-planning edicts. Tensions remained high, nearly a week after thousands clashed with police over an official campaign that residents say included forced abortions, property destruction, and arrests aimed at violators of the so-called "one-child policy."

*Chapter Ten*
# Finding Tranquility Amidst the Chaos

*"The task becomes how to convert time into eternity, how to fill our time with spirit: Six days a week we wrestle with the world, wringing profit from the earth; on the Sabbath we especially care for the seed of eternity planted in the soul. The world has our hands, but our soul belongs to Someone Else."*

(Rabbi Abraham Joshua Heschel, The Sabbath) [1]

*"I admire the Shabbat tradition, and no matter which faith you are of, there is nothing more wonderful than dedicating a certain day to spend time with your family and loved ones, absent of TV, phone, and other interruptions."*

(Joyce Giraud, Puerto Rican actress) [2]

*"Religion is the opium of the people."*

(Karl Marx) [3]

The brain behind Communism, Karl Marx in his avowedly secular approach to reorganizing society, ridiculed belief in God, as was mainly represented by Judaism and Christianity. Religion, Marx held, was a significant hindrance to reason, inherently masking the truth and misguiding followers, and was a significant force for maintaining the status quo that he was hoping to overthrow. Furthermore, Marx viewed religion as a tool of social control used by the bourgeoisie to keep the proletariat content with an unequal status quo. [4]

How fascinating that is, given the fact that

Communism's God-less and soul-less view of the world did not succeed in answering people's nagging existential, moral questions – not in the Soviet Union, not in Cuba, and certainly not in Communist China. Even though Marxism and other forms of dogmatic secularism have gained popularity among American youth in recent years, there is no logical reason why that spiritual failure will be any different in America, despite the entry into the White House of a Democrat president in 2021 and the ascendance of the radical Left in that party.

In chaotic times, wise people look for solace in tried-and-true traditions that have been passed down from generation to generation. Others look to their families for support, but also for comfort in times of crisis, and these have certainly been chaotic times, with the promise of more to come. In the United States, the economic and health impact from the Covid-19 pandemic, combined with the polarization and the havoc orchestrated by the violence of left-wing radicals, has fomented terrible uncertainty and rising anxiety in people's lives.

We spoke earlier about the importance of the family in imbuing in children the values of hard work, perseverance, and faith. Those values have to come from somewhere, and when we examine the backgrounds of successful people, there is almost always someone in the family who had a values-based impact on that person during childhood.

During this time, millions of American young adults have moved back in with their parents. In fact, a Zillow analysis on current population data from the US Census Bureau found that a record 32 million adults were living with their parents or grandparents in April 2020, and of those who have recently moved back home, many of them are adult members of Generation Z. [5]

While many would admit to financial strain stemming from job loss as a major factor, there are other factors having more to do with comfort and with the emotional security of family. Even if some consider it "politically incorrect" these days to talk about the value of the traditional family, it is highly unlikely that the pull to return home in such chaotic times is purely financial. And it is not just about the long-term impact of the Corona pandemic. These are, indeed, times of great uncertainty. Riots in the street, invasion of private businesses, and vandalism of public spaces, along with the skyrocketing crime rates as police forces are defunded; all of these are unnerving situations, wherever one stands politically, and however one relates to the bedlam in the streets, or tries to understand its root causes.

For adults choosing to relocate back to their parents' home, Lara Fielding, a clinical psychologist and author of Mastering Adulthood said:

*"The most natural thing in the world is to want to bond and affiliate with our safe cohort during this time ... It's the desire for familiarity. Right now, there is so much uncertainty, and that's the biggest stressor for most people. It is the 'most natural thing in the world' to crave familial comfort..."* [6]

Even though the family is so central in our lives, most of the articles about young adults moving back home speak about how difficult it is to get along with each other, which raises more general questions about the state of the American family and why family members can't seem to manage together.

As one article described the phenomenon:

*"Many others are returning to their childhood bedrooms and setting up workstations in the dining room of homes where food – and support – are in ample supply. The trade-off is often living in a household where siblings are sleeping nearby, and families are trying to figure out who will do a video conference from what room."* [7]

Yes, every family has its personality issues, its baggage, and its unresolved issues, but when moving back home is only about financial decisions and sharing of workspace, could it be that something was missing before the young adults moved out? Could it be that there is a much more general problem when families no longer eat together, except on one or two holidays in the course of a year, and even then, the intense political arguments get in the way of the turkey and cranberry sauce? Furthermore, could it be that there is a much deeper problem when time "shared" together is often with computers in front and cell phones in hand?

Maybe families need to go back to eating together on a regular basis. Research suggests that when a family eats together, they feel a strong bond with one another. Everyone leads disconnected lives at work and school, and this time allows them to reconnect. For the youngest family members, sharing a dinner at the table with parents helps promote language skills as you talk with them, and your partner, about the day. It also helps them develop patience and dexterity through the use of utensils, and it helps them develop social skills that include manners and taking turns. Perhaps if many of the young "revolutionaries" attacking the police today had some of that, they would be calmer, more content, and better-adjusted young adults.

One study, published in the *Pediatrics* journal, found

that kids who regularly enjoyed family meals were less likely to experience symptoms of depression and less likely to get into drug use. [8] The calmness and sense of security that comes from that special time together really makes a difference in a child's emotional well-being and self-confidence.

The National Center on Addiction and Substance Abuse at Columbia University has done a series of studies on the importance of family meals. One showed that kids who eat with their family less than three times a week were twice as likely to report receiving Cs or worse in school. Kids who ate with family five to seven times per week did much better, reporting mostly As and Bs. [9]

One area of focus for many mental health professionals is the issue of self-esteem. The security provided by regularly breaking bread as a family can help children feel more confident in themselves, according to experts at Stanford Children's Health, a pediatric health-care system affiliated with Stanford Medicine and Stanford University. By encouraging your children to talk about their day (and genuinely listening to their responses), you are communicating that you value and respect who they are. Children should be allowed to choose their own seats and encouraged to assist with chores associated with dinnertime, whether setting the table, serving the food, or cleaning up.

Finally, there are social benefits to that family bonding time. A 2018 Canadian study that followed a group of children from infancy through childhood found that participants whose families had positive meal experiences at age six showed a range of positive benefits by age ten. Besides general health and fitness, the social interaction and discussions of current issues at the table can make kids better communicators, noted the study's supervisor, Université de Montréal psychoeducation professor Linda Pagani, in a *Science Daily* interview. [10]

While all of these reasons for families eating together are important, the Sabbath, known to Jewish families as Shabbat or Shabbos, has many additional benefits that transcend just the positive features of family meals cited above.

For one thing, there is a total weekly focus on being with the family and sometimes with friends. The Sabbath is what many have called an "island in time," a twenty-five hour gap at the end of the week that is devoted to worshipping God and learning from the inspiring teachings in the Torah and its commentaries, which are, indeed, a guidebook for life. The focus is on studying those time-proven values in a relaxed and supportive environment. Jewish families around the world, whatever their ethnic backgrounds, racial backgrounds, or countries of origin are known to spend much time on that special day each week in prayer, while, at the same time, reconnecting with loved ones in a more relaxed, non-technology driven environment.

As one well-known convert to Judaism describes it:

*"We observe the Sabbath ... From Friday to Saturday we don't do anything but hang out with one another. We do not make phone calls. We are pretty observant, more than some, less than others. It's been such a great life decision for me. I am very modern, but I'm also a very traditional person, and I think that's an interesting juxtaposition in how I was raised as well. I really find that with Judaism, it creates an amazing blueprint for family connectivity."*

(Ivanka Trump) [11]

**Welcoming the Sabbath:** A Jewish woman in Jerusalem says the blessing over the Sabbath candles and recites a special Sabbath prayer for her family.

Given what we know about the hard-working Trump family, whatever one's political leanings may be, one can appreciate that ability to "tune out" from the work world, and to turn the full focus to the immediate family unit. We have already discussed earlier the lofty virtue of hard work. Without it, we achieve nothing in life, and, as we have seen, we can go far if we are willing to set goals and do everything we can to achieve them, even if we have to sweat and sacrifice a tremendous amount to get there. When one wants to achieve and is willing to sacrifice, and sometimes even suffer for it, the Jewish experience has taught us that no amount of discrimination can stop us.

Even so, work is what we do all week, but as humans, we also need time to refuel, to take a break, to relax, and to regroup. When one does that with loved ones, it has been proven to have lasting value. All week long, we are bound to the material and technological world and are, in a sense, slaves to its pressures. Throughout our work week, we are, in essence, asserting our dominance over nature, exploiting it, preferably without harming it too much, but we actually become dependent on its abundance, essentially a slave to it. On the Sabbath, we are freed from this slavery. We can exist in harmony with our world, while enjoying its bounty, but we also reconnect with the world of the spirit. [12]

All week long, we are ruled by our need to dominate the world. People are usually defined by their occupations. One is a plumber, another a nurse, a construction worker, a salesman, a teacher, a computer technician, a journalist, or a housewife. A person's occupation is, in fact, the way in which he or she exercises dominance over the world. Yet somehow, his or her most basic humanity is submerged by the chosen occupation.

On the Sabbath, all that is changed, everything is transformed. Every man is a king, every woman a queen, ruling his or her destiny, no longer defined and dictated to by the world of work. When there are children involved, they follow the parents' lead as princes and princesses in the family unit. [13]

Orthodox, or religiously observant, Jews enjoy a full day of rest, worship, and family engagement from

Friday evening to Saturday night. This is a worldwide phenomenon, but visitors to Israel immediately notice the peace and uplifting serenity of a Shabbat in Jerusalem. There is nothing comparable to the transformation from the hustle-bustle of a busy Friday morning in Jerusalem to the Friday evening calm and tranquility from sunset onward until sundown on Saturday.

**Sabbath Peace in Israel:** There is perhaps nothing as peaceful as a Shabbat night stroll, near the Old City walls in Jerusalem. As we greet each other in Israel, "Shabbat Shalom!"

The busy work week, the busy leisure and shopping weekend, is essentially set aside for an entire day. There are no computers, no televisions, and no cell phones in use; we live momentarily on an island in time when all attention is focused on the family, along with the teachings of the Torah and its relevant commentaries that confront the important moral questions in our lives. We discuss these issues at the table, along with more personal conversation. It truly is a day when people actually eat together, sing together, and talk to each other in a relaxed, direct way, without sending text messages![14]

**Extending the Warmth of the Sabbath Day:** Joined by young family members at home, immediately after the conclusion of Shabbat, Israeli musician Shlomo Katz "extends" the special day with the musical Havdalah ceremony.

Aside from the minority of the American Jewish population that observes the Sabbath day, there was a time when most Americans of all faiths were given a full day of rest and reflection that was observed by almost all families. That day was usually Sunday, not the day prescribed in the Bible, and the day was conducted according to the Christian understanding of the concept, but it was designated as a day for rest, family, and worship. Sunday was once a relatively quiet day in America when most stores were closed, and even required to be closed. Perhaps, in some towns in the United States, it is still like that, and there are some Christian families that have maintained the tradition in some way, but to a great extent, the Sabbath concept has been lost. In today's America, it is either work, leisure, or shopping, with no full day of rest from the busy technological world, except for those who choose, of their own free will, to observe the Sabbath.

The Puritans were probably the first to enforce the Blue Laws or Sunday Laws on the North American continent, banning many commercial and recreational activities on Sundays during the 1600s. Colonial America observed Sunday as a day of rest in the 18th century as well, and established laws governing its observance. These laws carried over as the new country was formed. Within twelve years of the framing of the constitution, many states had Sunday Laws in effect that outlawed working, traveling, and selling goods on that day ... It was not the Jewish Sabbath, but it was a time to have a break from work and commerce, and a respite from the rushed, high pressured atmosphere associated with those important parts of our lives. [15]

The importance of the Judeo-Christian heritage in providing solace and family bonding in times of uncertainty and chaos cannot be underestimated. Therefore, it was disturbing that in the height of the Covid-19 crisis, when many of America's Democrat governors and mayors shut down places of worship, they simultaneously allowed the massive rioting and looting to continue. The hypocrisy in the policy was shocking and could only be interpreted as a strategy to cancel the traditionally religious, or more conservative voices, while allowing, even encouraging the voices and the turmoil of the radical Left to congregate in large numbers. Apparently, the fact that they were attacking police officers and store owners, setting fire to government buildings, and destroying national monuments wasn't problematic to the self-righteous Democrat politicians.

After all, in the eyes of the secular Left, the real problem wasn't the contagion from Covid-19. The real problem was the political threat from those weekly gatherings of pesky worshippers who didn't support the Left's secular agenda, especially their promotion of late-term abortions and of gay marriage as an ideal lifestyle, their dogmatic opposition to school choice, and of course, their opposition to traditional organized religious worship, such as the Jewish Sabbath tradition, or the Christian tradition of going to church on Sunday morning and then having a nice lunch and family time.

Obviously, most Americans are not Jewish and do not need to do it like we do, but wouldn't it be healthy to slow down a bit, and infuse some of these more grounded traditional elements into the hectic, materialistic, and technologically heavy lifestyle? Especially in these chaotic times, when cities are burning and dangerous forces are trying to destroy the wonderful freedoms and values that Americans have always cherished, an island in time may give a little peace and clarity of mind, before the battles to come.

*Chapter Eleven*

# Confronting the Revolution

*"All animals are equal, but some animals are more equal than others."*

(George Orwell, Animal Farm) [1]

George Orwell's brilliance was in his ability to describe what most perceptive Americans already know to be true, but that the naive young Americans following the radical groups have yet to grasp. The hypocrisy of the radical Left lies in the reality that if given power, they will create a new tyranny far worse than that which the Founders thought they had left behind some 250 years ago. Orwell describes how the so-called "anti-fascists" (as in today's Antifa) eventually prove themselves to be the real fascists, shutting down free speech and physically assaulting opponents.

In his masterpiece novel, "Animal Farm," the revolutionary leader of what has become the ruling pigs, the aptly titled Napoleon, along with his pig cohorts, become indistinguishable from the "evil capitalist" human farmers that they had overthrown, just as Stalin and the Russian communists eventually became indistinguishable from the aristocrats whom they had replaced and the Western capitalists whom they had denounced. [2]

We have already discussed the difficult reality Americans are facing, in which the streets of many cities are literally burning, but this really is but a symptom of a much greater malaise that is afflicting this great nation. A significant portion of the American population, especially the young, tragically has never learned its history and the redeeming values on which it was founded. The educational system, especially at the college level, has been hijacked by Marxist revisionists who have been presenting a distorted view of American history focusing mainly on past flaws, such as slavery and discrimination against women, while ignoring the elements of context and correction. Therefore, the young naive Americans, many of whom are even embarrassed to call themselves Americans, see the United States as an evil force in the world and foolishly think that the Marxist groups will provide the perfect system with no racism, no sexism, no Homophobia, no Islamophobia, in short, a gender-free society of bliss and something called "social justice." This new-age "movement" will provide them with a cause, a sense of purpose in their angry young lives, that perhaps will resemble an uglier version of the romanticized 1960s that their parents once lived through. Never mind that anti-Semitism is also featured prominently in this movement. Some explain that away by saying that they are "only" anti-Israel, as if hatred of the one tiny Jewish state is not synonymous with anti-Semitism.

They are being taught by the leaders of this movement to see capitalism as a cruel economic system, to believe that the traditions of Judeo-Christian civilization are primitive, backward, and unenlightened, and to believe that the nuclear family is "gender-biased" and immoral. The goal is to undo the American system in whatever way possible. Creating havoc and fomenting turmoil are the carefully calculated means to the goal of a globalist, socialist, government-controlled society in which the freedoms that Americans hold dear, including the ability to think and communicate with each other, will be washed away like a politically correct tsunami.

It worked for Adolf Hitler, who took advantage of the economic and political chaos in between the two world wars to bring his National Socialist German Workers' (Nazi) Party to power through free elections, but leading to iron-fisted rule. [3]

While some would dispute Hitler's use of the word "socialist" as being inappropriate to describe his economic policies, the undisputable fact is that he fomented and exploited the chaos and instability in Germany to attain control and power. Chaos and instability are often the path to revolution.

The primary goal of the widespread Covid lockdowns that were carried out mainly by Democrat mayors and governors was not to defeat the virus. The goal was to severely damage the economy and create turmoil in the hope of defeating President Trump, who had built a roaring economy during his first three years in office, until the CCP virus hit the American shores. How convenient it was for the "protest" movement that has always thrived on anarchy, as the deserted streets and businesses soon were taken over by the mobs, who further ravaged the American economy with their rioting, with their looting, and their assault on the American system of law enforcement and justice.

For the results of this madness, take a look at the Big Apple, where violent crime rates had plummeted during the Giuliani years, with the low rates continuing into the Bloomberg years. New York City rose to great heights, but those days are over, as the days of appeasing lawless behavior and pandering to criminals, all in the name of social justice of course, have taken over. With a rapid wave of subway attacks and shootings, violent crime is soaring in New York City. Well before the end of 2020, citywide shootings had already nearly doubled – from 698 in 2019 to 1,359 in 2020 as of November 15, according to NYPD figures. Shooting victims have more than doubled, from 828 during all of 2019 to 1,667 in 2020 through November 15, and there were already 405 homicide victims, compared to 295 in the previous year. This pointless anarchy was the natural result of the organized anarchy that the radicals planned through their "protests." [4]

Even one week before the November 2020 presidential election, the entire wild scene of riots and looting was replayed again, this time in Philadelphia, after another (black) armed suspect was shot and killed by a (white) police officer for refusing to drop his weapon. The suspect, Walter Wallace, 27, an aspiring rapper, had often rhymed about shooting people, including police officers, and was awaiting trial for threatening to shoot a woman. He also had previously kicked down the door of another woman and allegedly held a gun to her head, according to media reports.

Court records revealed that the suspect had a substantial criminal history. In 2017, he pleaded guilty to robbery, assault and possessing an instrument of crime, according to documents obtained by Fox News. The rioting and looting that followed this event set Philadelphia on fire for several days with over one thousand looters rampaging through stores in the Port Richmond section of the city. The rioting throngs who attacked police officers were armed with bricks. Meanwhile, the evening news shows were highlighting

Wallace's kids talking about what a wonderful guy their father was. [5]

The radical left-wing mobs in Philadelphia, as in many other places, expressed the growing anti-Semitism of the Left.

A number of Jewish participants at one of the BLM-organized "protests" in Philadelphia were surrounded, and told to "go home," as one of the members of the radical Black Hebrews group (black, but definitely not Hebrews, nor Jews) that was threatening them, made reference to what he called "the synagogue of Satan," an anti-Semitic slur that had been made famous by the noted Muslim Jew-hater and racist, Louis Farrakhan. One bully from the threatening group was heard asking, "Amalek, what y'all doing down here? You don't live here," giving these frightened Jews, the odd label of the Amalek tribe, possibly the worst Biblical enemy of the Jewish people. One of the stunned Jewish protesters was heard pleading with them, saying, "We're just showing solidarity," but it didn't help as they were again surrounded by the crowd, shoved, and told to "Get the f*** out!" [6]

However, the leftist violence was certainly not just directed at Jews. These scenes continued after the November election, as well. On November 14, tens of thousands of Trump supporters enthusiastically gathered in the streets of Washington, DC to demonstrate support for the President and his claims of massive election fraud resulting from Democrat exploitation of the mail-in voting.

*"Those who vote decide nothing. Those who count the vote decide everything."*

(Joseph Stalin, Soviet Communist dictator) [7]

There were hours of peaceful protests by pro-Trump supporters, and these were genuinely peaceful protests, unlike those in the Capitol two months later. In these November 14 protests, there was absolutely no rioting, no looting, no attacks on police or on national monuments. Furthermore, there were no rocks or Molotov cocktails thrown at government buildings. Then came the thugs of Antifa and BLM mobs after dark when the crowds had thinned out, who lynched and assaulted individual protestors as they were walking through the streets of the capital wearing MAGA hats or simply just walking through the streets. Trump supporters were sucker-punched, kicked in the head while already on the ground, had eggs thrown at them and were doused with unknown liquids. The DC police force struggled to contain and disperse the mobs, eventually making several arrests in the process, but not before at least one badly bloodied Trump supporter was left on the ground after being lynched by the mobs. [8]

In a separate incident that evening, a slew of fireworks was set off in a restaurant where a small group of Trump supporters were having dinner on the patio. Needless to say, chaos ensued, and more arrests were made. [9]

These assaults weren't a political reaction to the president. Joe Biden had already been declared president by all of the major news networks. It was simply a continuation of the intimidation process being carried out by the radical Left. Innocent peaceful civilians were brutally assaulted, while Biden's silence, Kamala Harris's silence, and that of their Democrat comrades was deafening.

Kelley Paul, wife of Sen. Rand Paul (R-Ky), weighed in on the violence that took place against the Trump

**The Cancel Culture Shuts Her Down:** Black-hooded Klan-like thugs attack an older woman, stealing and destroying her Trump-Pence flag. This is, of course, a violent assault on her rights of freedom of speech and freedom of expression. Liberals, by definition, believe in open-mindedness. These human vermin, who Joe Biden says are "just an idea", are not liberals. In reality, the "anti-fascists" are the real fascists.

supporters and said what she saw "brings back awful memories" that she and her husband experienced during the Republican National Convention.

Following the hostile altercation, Mrs. Paul called out Politico for appearing to downplay the incident by saying "Protesters confront Rand Paul outside White House after RNC." [10]

"No @politico, we were not 'confronted' by protestors. We were circled by a hateful mob shouting vile expletives, preventing us from moving," wrote Mrs. Paul.

Senator Paul tweeted, "I promise you that at least some of the members and the people who attacked us were not from D.C., they flew here on a plane, they all have fresh new clothes and they were paid to be here," Paul said. "It is a crime to do that and it needs to be traced. The FBI needs to investigate." Much to his dismay, Paul was later told that the FBI would not investigate. [11]

Could these violent scenes have occurred under a Democrat administration? The short answer is yes, absolutely. Occupy Wall Street emerged during the Obama administration, the Ferguson riots erupted during the Obama years, and Obama cheered them all on. So, too, have other left-wing Dems more recently praised, or, in the conspicuous case of Biden, ignored the more recent riots, apparently believing that "the fight for social justice" and the new social world order has many players with many different roles.

The violent Antifa mobs that Biden has consistently refused to condemn have their role to play, as well, in the radicals' revolution. Just as the Cossack mobs and the Nazi Brown Shirts mobs assaulted Jews years ago in Europe, and just as the Ku Klux Klan attacked blacks in the South, today it is Antifa, the "anti-fascist" Fascists, who sadly, seem to be evolving into the domestic terrorist arm of the Democrat party of Biden and Harris. If they don't approve of the violence, why are they silent?

Unless the mainstream of America wakes up and acts quickly, everything that Orwell had predicted will come to fruition, probably in an even more nefarious and violent form than what was seen in the former Soviet Union or what we are seeing today in Cuba, in North Korea, or in Communist China.

It is not too late to stop the step-by-step revolution that the activists from the radical Left groups have been organizing. We in Israel have learned certain lessons in the roller coaster ride that we call Jewish history, both from our successes in confronting the challenges, and from our mistakes. These lessons can be summarized in ten suggestions that can be useful in countering the anti-American revolutionaries, who have essentially declared unofficial war on the American values that made the United States the leader of the free world, a nation that is still admired around the world:

**Understand that Nothing is Irreversible** – Even though Supreme Court decisions, as well as government decisions, are often based on precedent, there is nothing that cannot be reversed, unless such a reversal violates the Constitution, as originally written. It is important to understand this basic principle, but it is also critical to understand that the reversal of deleterious change in certain fields such as education requires much more planning, time, and perseverance than in others, since the Left has methodically engineered those changes quietly behind the scenes for the past several decades.

**Believe What They Say to Each Other** – If you want to understand what the radicals really believe, listen carefully to what they say to each other, not to you and not through carefully selected media and lawyers. For years, we in Israel have listened to the Palestinians, ever since they established their "peoplehood," back in 1964. We listened first to Yasser Arafat and then Mahmoud Abbas talking about peace in English, while in Arabic, they called for Jihad, or "holy war," while occasionally slipping up and revealing themselves in English, as well. For many years, Israel's left-leaning leaders put their heads in the proverbial Middle East sand and ignored such doublespeak, or rationalized it away. Dear Americans, beware and be careful not to look at your enemies through rose-colored glasses. Listen carefully to what they say to their own ideological kin. If the marching radicals chant to their mobs, "Kill the f_ _ _ ing police," as they have in numerous American cities, you should believe it. They would not chant those words to their people if it were not what they intended to do.

**Do Not Tolerate Violence** – If you give an inch, they will take a mile. We have recently seen that principle played out in real time in American cities. If you accept verbal mob violence against law enforcement officers, it will soon become physical attacks on police with buckets of water, as was seen in New York City. Once that is permitted, it will lead to rocks and Molotov cocktails, the so-called minimal violence. The mobs will take note of what they can get away with and up the ante every time. Harassing and assaulting the police, violently attacking their ideological opponents, looting stores, defacing monuments, taking control of neighborhoods, and setting government buildings on fire are just intermediate goals, but as long as they see that they can commit such crimes and get away with them, they will attempt more daring violent acts against the symbols of American government and society all the way to the White House.

Stop it in its tracks and never respond to the violence of the leftist rioters by rioting yourselves. The lawlessness in the Capitol building in DC on January 6, 2021, was an unacceptable one-time event. The apparent fact that extremists from BLM or neo-Nazi types [12] were there inciting violence and other unlawful acts doesn't justify anyone else's participation in what was clearly against the law. It also is not justified by the fact that, for an entire year, the media and the Democrat leadership ignored, or even praised and raised funds for the rioting mobs of the Left. True, conservatives have been frustrated, because no one wants to be a human doormat or a human punching bag, but don't ever stoop down to their level by being violent and/or unlawful yourselves.

Always keep your cool, get organized, and start doing the quiet, strategic things that make a real difference. The radicals have been doing it smoothly for decades. It's time for conservatives to reverse the process by adopting a determined, methodical proactive approach on all levels – restoring conservative values to the public and higher education systems, using the sane media, getting active politically, and most importantly, teaching those values within your own family.

**Cut off the Funding** – When the rioters and looters were going berserk in the streets of New York City, there were piles of bricks on the street corners of midtown Manhattan. Those piles did not materialize from magic. They came from somewhere and they were funded from somewhere. Could the baseball bats and helmets of the Antifa battle gear be an indication of the source? When the rioters were creating havoc in Louisville, Kentucky in September of 2020, many of them were seen methodically unloading riot equipment from a U-Haul truck. It did not float down from the sky. It came from somewhere. Similar well-organized and equipped Antifa-led riots have continued well into 2021, especially in Democrat-run cities like Denver, Seattle, and, of course, Portland.

In Israel, steps have been taken recently in the Israeli Knesset (Parliament) to block foreign funding that undermines the State of Israel and its national institutions. It would be wise for the Congress and the administration to research and hopefully block sources of funding that act to undermine the United States and its national institutions. Our challenge in Israel comes from foreign governments and radical billionaires like George Soros who fund NGOs that seek to undermine the existence of the State of Israel. Sounds familiar? The big-money donors do it quietly, but they are also attempting to overthrow the American way of life by funding groups like BLM and Antifa that are working methodically through a multi-pronged assault on American symbols, which as we all know too well, has included violent rioting, intimidation, and destruction as a way of life. This heavy funding can be stopped through carefully crafted legislation, followed by enforcement.

Do not allow the United States to become like Malmo, Sweden, where, over several decades, a once delightful seaport city was gradually turned into a haven for violent Muslim radicals. Beyond what was witnessed briefly in Seattle, many neighborhoods in Malmo have become permanent CHAZ zones where police dare not tread for fear of igniting riots by their very presence. Lawlessness and fear have become the rule rather than the exception. CHAZ in Seattle was only a small taste of things to come.

The heavy funding given to violent revolutionary organizations must be stopped at the source. Cut off the many millions of dollars in funding from George Soros's foundations for BLM and Antifa. [13] Cut off the funding given by corporations like IBM, Airbnb, Cisco, Reddit, and Uber (only a very partial list), that reap fortunes from doing business in the free marketplace of the USA, but openly support BLM's violence. [14] Cut off the funding given by confused, arrogant Hollywood stars like Seth Rogen, Steve Carell, Jameela Jamil, and Patton Oswalt (here, too, only a partial list), who supported the violence through their financial support for the radical Minnesota Freedom Fund, but refused appeals to support the victims of the riots and the looting. [15]

The violence will not end until the sources of funding are blocked. Yes, we all have the right to give donations freely, but no, we do not have the right to exploit that very freedom to finance violent insurrection against the nation that grants that freedom.

**Take Back the Universities** – There is no area in which the radical Left has been more successful in accomplishing its goals than in the field of education. When Bill Ayers, the former leader of the radical

**Raising New Young Radicals:** 1960's radical Bill Ayers, one of former President Barack Obama's mentors, has moved on from bombing government buildings to teaching the youth about socialism and inciting them about the evils of America. Thousands of radical leftist educators have infiltrated the higher education system, benefitting from the freedoms that the American system provides in order to destroy it.

Weather Underground group in the 1960s, was revealed as having been pivotal in launching young Barack Obama's political career, there was some minimal political commotion, mainly in the more conservative media, with a focus on understanding the actual views of the soon-to-be-elected President Obama. What was less discussed was the fact that Bill Ayers for many years had already been Professor Bill Ayers. Yes, it is true that Ayers' claim to fame was that he and his cohorts had bombed the Pentagon, but Ayers eventually seemed to "go establishment," becoming a professor of elementary education, but with an agenda to radically change the educational system. From 1995 to 1999, Obama led an education foundation called the Chicago Annenberg Challenge (CAC), and remained on the board until 2001. The group poured more than $100 million into the hands of community organizers and radical education activists. The CAC was the brainchild of Professor Ayers, but it should be emphasized that he is only one of many "establishment radicals." [16]

The infiltration of the leftist radicals into the higher education system and the encroaching dominance of secularism and the growing admiration for Socialism/Marxism throughout that system is the most systemic danger to American civilization that there could be. Furthermore, the attempts to teach a revisionist history in the universities and to turn conservatives into campus outcasts are succeeding. Those parents who are frightened by this trend would be well advised to stop sending their children to these "halls of learning" until real changes are made towards tolerance and inclusion of conservative ideas, and to support the building of alternative institutions that are more faithful to the concepts and the values that built America. Last, but not least, act through your political representatives to stop all government funding for these fat institutions that fund left-wing radicalism and are the epitome of intolerance towards the free exchange of ideas.

**Educate the Children** – One of the saddest results of the persistent, ongoing efforts to secularize and radicalize America has been the gradual transformation of the public school system. I remember growing up in America and attending New York public schools, in which we pledged allegiance to the flag, learned lessons about the great American heroes like George Washington, Benjamin Franklin, and Abraham Lincoln,

**One Nation Under God:** Love for country is a value that has to be nurtured in children from a young age. Pledging allegiance to God and country as a sacred value, along with lessons about American heroes, can help restore the sense of pride to the American nation.

and learned about the important values of honesty and hard work. Schools are not just places where we learn to read and write. In the loftiest sense, schools are trusted partners that support parents in the raising of their children and the instilling of those great Biblical values like honoring parents, not coveting what is not yours, and being respectful to others. Do not leave that sacred task in the hands of radical anarchists. Act through political, legal, and other means to restore the educational system to what it once was – a vast school system that more accurately reflects the great values of Judeo-Christian civilization. Meanwhile, it would be wise to support the school choice movement, which will help to restore competition and thus increase excellence in all of the schools. It will also restore to parents the right to decide if they really want their children to be educated by radical secularists whose spiritual, ethical guidebook often seems to be the Communist Manifesto.

Get involved with your local PTA and make your voices heard. Run for your local school board. Vote for your local school board, whether you have children in the schools or not. Influence change from within. The radical Left has been doing it for decades. Get involved and fight for your values!

**Restore the Traditional American Family** – With all due respect to the Supreme Court, and without being too descriptive, God created Man and Woman to procreate and build a family together. That is the ideal. Yes, it is a fact that there are other family structures that exist, and even succeed, through the efforts of remarkable individuals, but they are not the ideal, as Secretary of Housing and Urban Development, Dr. Ben Carson, who we spoke about earlier, and who benefitted from an amazing mother, would probably attest to. Fathers and mothers are not the same, often acting like they are from other planets, but ideally, that very fact helps them to complement each other and ultimately work together, because that it how God made us. Recognizing those differences, not ignoring them, nor trying to transform gender identity into some amorphic bubble of confusion, is the key that helps parents to valiantly work together to have a successful family life.

In most modern Orthodox Jewish families, especially in Israel, the values are very traditional, yet wives have careers outside the home, but the family always comes first. Contrary to public stereotypes, most of the fathers in those often-large families would also agree that the family comes first. Therefore, they play an active role in the chores of family life, a modern family-based philosophy that the recently confirmed Supreme Court Justice Amy Coney Barrett and her husband Jesse would certainly agree with, as they both lead productive careers, but their seven children (including their two adopted children) come first. They are Catholic, I am Jewish, but we would all agree that the traditional family is the core of what has made Judeo-Christian civilization great. Flexible partnership in the age of female career accomplishment can make the embattled nuclear family stronger, as long as husband and wife are in full coordination and working together. That being said, a mother (or even a father) who decides to stay at home full-time for at least a number of years, should not be shamed. There is no greater task than to devote oneself to family life. Either Americans will learn to value that treasure in the coming years, or the society will rapidly collapse.

**Never Apologize for Saying that All Lives Matter** – It is wrong to combat racism with racism. Forced quotas, often called "affirmative action," are racist. The expression, "white privilege," which lumps all white people in one evil basket, is in and of itself racist. As we in Israel have learned from the challenging absorption of our disadvantaged brethren from poor countries like Yemen, India, and Ethiopia, there are times when special help is needed, but turning it into a racially based program of hand-outs is in and of itself racist. Therefore, demanding reparations from all white people alive today for past slavery generations ago is absolutely racist, as well as non-productive, since it teaches no life and work skills, but only gives monetary handouts. Yes, black lives do matter, and that's why those who need help, whatever their race, but including black people, should be provided with help and guidance that will lead to strong families, education without a lowering of standards, and equal opportunity for all. Even so, it should be based on need, not on race. All lives matter, and judging people based on race is, indeed, racist, no matter which race we are referring to.

No one said it better than Dr. Martin Luther King Jr.: "I have a dream that my four little children will one day live in a nation where they will not be judged by the color of their skin, but by the content of their character." [17]

Let us honor that noble dream and that legacy. All of us.

**Use the Media Wisely** – Much of the mainstream media in America has abandoned all pretense of objectivity in its coverage of the "protests." Cable networks like CNN and MSNBC happily have taken on roles as cheerleaders for the left-wing movements, and as aggressive critics of anyone who has dared to point out that the emperors creating bedlam in the streets have no clothes, that the "spontaneous anti-racism protest movement" is actually a burgeoning multi-faceted leftist revolution in the making. Speaking of the emperor having no clothes, Big-Tech media giants like Twitter and Facebook were recently caught with their pants down, in a bald-faced attempt to censor all coverage of the Joe Biden-Hunter Biden China, Russia, and Ukraine corruption scandal. Thousands of Hunter Biden email correspondences were discovered shortly before the November 2020 presidential election, exposing the former vice president's involvement in a thirty-year-long racketeering and influence peddling scandal.

In a brazen act of censorship revealing obvious political bias, just three weeks before Election Day, Twitter blocked the accounts of the NY Post and the Trump Campaign immediately after the Post broke the story. The thought police that Orwell wrote about are already here.

Two months later, after the unfortunate event at the Capitol, Twitter permanently blocked President Trump's account, while continuing to allow full freedom of speech for Iran's dictator Ayatollah Ali Khamenei, Venezuelan Socialist President Nicolas Maduro, Muslim anti-Semitic preacher Louis Farrakhan, and anti-Semitic Congresswomen Ilhan Omar, and Rashida Tlaib. All of these individuals have posted violent posts that include hate speech and anti-Semitism and/or openly incite rioting and killing. [18]

The new world of Big-Tech is frightening, and indeed, very Orwellian. The potential for massive thought control surpasses the former Soviet Union and more closely resembles that of the Communist Party in China. As explained by Larry P. Arnn, president of Hillsdale College:

*"The old word 'science' comes from a Latin word meaning 'to know.' The new word 'technology' comes from a Greek word meaning 'to make.' The transition from traditional to modern science means that we are not so much seeking to know when we study nature as seeking to make things – and ultimately, to remake nature itself. That spirit of remaking nature – including human nature – greatly emboldens both human beings and governments. Imbued with that spirit, and employing the tools of modern science, totalitarianism is a form of government that reaches farther than tyranny and attempts to control the totality of things."* [19]

This blatant overreach of power, leading to the rise of tyranny and totalitarianism in the age of Big-Tech monopolies, and with the proud collusion of the radicalized Democrats, is what we are seeing today.

Within hours of the permanent banning of Trump's Twitter account, several million Americans protested the censorship by moving over to relatively new social media app Parler. The reaction of the establishment media radicals at Google, Apple, and Amazon was quick in coming, as the Big-Tech giants continued their purge by banning Parler from their app stores, in an obvious attempt to shut them down completely.

Furthermore, in another shocking capitulation to the thought police, Simon & Schuster announced on January 7, 2021, that it would no longer publish a planned book by Senator Josh Hawley, one of the Republican lawmakers who led objections to Congress certifying President-elect Joe Biden's victory. Senator Hawley responded, "This could not be more Orwellian. Simon & Schuster is canceling my contract because I was representing my constituents, leading a debate on the Senate floor on voter integrity, which they now have decided to redefine as sedition. Let me be clear, this is not just a contract dispute. It's a direct assault on the 1st Amendment. Only approved speech can now be published. This is the Left looking to cancel everyone they don't approve of. I will fight this cancel culture with everything I have." [20]

Yes, the thought police that Orwell warned us about are already here, but they have been here before, in Israel as well.

On November 4, 1995, in the midst of a deeply polarized political climate, Israeli Prime Minister Yitzhak Rabin was assassinated. His murder took place with the backdrop of many loud, but peaceful demonstrations and protests against the controversial Oslo Accords, which Rabin had strongly supported and pushed forward, in the naive hope that appeasing the Palestinians with autonomy would lead to peace. The suspected murderer of Rabin was eventually convicted and sent to jail for life.

Even so, in the weeks and months after the assassination, the murder was exploited by the radical Left to label Likud leader and future Prime Minister Benjamin Netanyahu as responsible for incitement, and even labeled him a murderer. In fact, the entire Right was panned in the left-leaning media and the accusations against conservative politicians were coming fast and furious. If you had opposed Oslo, you were labeled an accomplice to murder. Netanyahu seemed to be on the defensive for years, as the relentless attacks seemed at times, to leave him on the ropes with no will to fight back. He was elected prime minister in a close election for his first term in 1996, but temporarily left politics after being defeated badly in 1999. He gradually made his political comeback several years later, eventually becoming the longest serving prime minister in Israel's history. The Right, which had been so brutally maligned in the terrible aftermath of the assassination, has also recovered and has gradually become an assertive and powerful force in Israeli politics, but to this day, Netanyahu often seems to be looking over his shoulder, for fear of what the Left might say about him.

Trump has certainly made mistakes, as have many conservatives, but the Israeli experience teaches us that one must stand firm and act boldly, using the media wisely. The steps taken must be strategically planned out in the fields of education, media, and law. It must be absolutely peaceful with no violence at all, but never back down under the relentless assaults of the Left, which knows exactly what it's doing in its attempts to stifle free speech on one side of the aisle. Once the thought police become official, as in Orwell's "1984," all will be lost, so never be afraid to speak your mind and act on your beliefs, while you still can. The best defense is a good offense. Strongly assertive, but peaceful. As in sports, in politics, as well.

To stop the biased media onslaught:

1. Do not watch the fake media unless you need to in order to point out falsehood.

2. Support legitimate honest media vocally and financially, if needed and if you can.
3. Get personally and professionally involved in media if you have the talent.
4. Voice your opinions and expose bias in every legal way possible.
5. If you have the ability, establish new media outlets, including on social media.
6. Ignore Twitter and all other biased social media that censor legitimate opinions that they disagree with. Move over to platforms that are not controlled by the thought police.

**Do Not Fear the G Word** – The dollar bill says the words "In God We Trust." The United States was founded mainly by religious Christians on a belief in God according to the Ten Commandments. The Torah tells us that God gave the Ten Commandments to Moses for the Israelite nation when they gathered at Mount Sinai. The Founders of the USA made those commandments the spiritual and social blueprint for their developing nation. Those guidelines for life spoke of

**In God We Trust:** The dollar bill with its slogan, "In God We Trust", should remind everyone of the religious foundations of the American nation, precious roots that are under attack.

honoring parents, keeping the Sabbath day, not coveting what does not belong to you, being honest, the sanctity of marriage, not murdering, not stealing, etc.

For the revolution of the radical Left to succeed, Judeo-Christian civilization must fall. The reverse is also true, so the real question is whether Americans are willing to fight for their country's values, or have they already been intimidated by the domestic terrorists and the verbal assault from the Left?

It's not too late for Americans to fight back before a great nation that has been a beacon of light for the world deteriorates into a vapid totalitarian country, in which words cannot be spoken, traditional families cannot stay together, and God cannot be worshipped freely without the contrary demands of the thought police.

In the words of the great Torah sage, Rabbi Hillel:

*"If I am not for myself, who will be for me? But if I am only for myself, who am I?" And if not now, when?"*
(Ethics of the Fathers 1:14)

Americans who care about themselves, but also about their families and their communities, and haven't become totally jaded and apathetic, must also care about their country and its freedoms as guaranteed in the Constitution. But are they really guaranteed? In the case of a revolution, whether a gradual, creeping revolution or a massive overthrow, those guarantees will be swept away with the winds of change.

The guarantees enshrined in the Constitution have to be defended and fought for, not just in the political realm, but also in the marketplace of ideas, which means in the media and in the schools, and, of course, in the courts. There are no shortcuts. Now is the time to get to work, before it's too late...

# Index

# Image Credits

*Cover*

**Washington, DC Protest:** Drew Angerer/Getty Images
**Israel Bus Bombing:** David Silverman/Getty Images

*Chapter One*

**Slavery in Egypt:** Bettmann / Contributor/Getty Images
**Seeing the Good in Everyone:** Visual Studies Workshop/Getty
**The Official Return to Jewish Sovereignty:** Wikipedia
**A Biblical Nation in the Middle East:** www.cia.gov
**God Put You in Your Mother's Womb:** Fritz Cohen/GPO/Getty Images
**Keeping the Promise:** US State Department
**Making America Tough Again:** AFP Photo/Saul Loeb/Getty Images

*Chapter Two*

**Warned of Thought Control:** Cassowary Colorizations / Wikimedia Common
**Not an Arab Spring:** Jaafar Ashtiyeh / AFP) via Getty Images
**The African Slave Trade:** Rischgitz/Getty Images
**Taken to America by Force:** Stefano Bianchetti/Corbis via Getty Images
**Tikun Olam** (Repairing the World): Hulton Archive/Getty Images
**Taken Captive by the Jordanian Army:** from "For The Sake Of Jerusalem" (Mazo Publishers, 2006).
**From Slavery to Freedom:** Thomas Coex / AFP via Getty Images

*Chapter Three*

**Guilty as Charged by the Tribunal:** Stephen Maturen/Getty Images
**Go Home Jacob, Go Home:** Stephen Maturen/Getty Images
**Shutting Down Macy's, Shutting Down Manhattan:** Scott Heins/ Getty Images
**Violence, Vandalism, and Shutdowns for the Radical Revolution:** Jason Redmond/AFP via Getty Images
**People's Republic of CHAZ:** David Ryder/Getty Images

*Chapter Four*

**No to Racism, No to Violence, No to Riots, No to Looting:** US Information Agency.

**Vulgarity & Vandalism & Defunding:** Ron Adar/SOPA Images/ LightRocket via Getty Images

**Sad Descent into Third-Worldism:** Roberto Schmidt/AFP/Getty

**In the Radicals' Ideology, Mothers and Daughters Become Legitimate Targets:** Musa Al-Shaer/AFP via Getty Images

**For the Revolution:** Hazem Bader/AFP via Getty Images)

**Burn the Israeli Police:** Oren Nahshon/AFP via Getty Images

**Murdered by a Rock Thrown at His Head:** The Shoham family

**"Itbach Al Yahud!":** Ilia Yefimovich/Getty Images

**American Radicals - Learning from their Palestinian Comrades:** David McNew/Getty Images

**Privileged Revolutionaries:** Wikimedia

### Chapter Five

**The Epitome of Appeasement:** Wikimedia

**Learn from Israel's Mistakes:** Israel GPO, Ohayon Avi

**Revolutionary Comrades:** Sovfoto/Universal Images Group via Getty Images

**Fighting Free Markets and Private Initiative:** Mario Tama/Getty Images

**Welcoming Only Legal Immigrants:** Nick Brundle Photography/ Getty Images

### Chapter Six

**Jerusalem Temple Warning:** Wikipedia

**Blowing the Great Trumpet:** Wikipedia

**Freeing the Slaves:** Francis Bicknell Carpenter

**From the Plantation to the Senate:** VCG Wilson/Corbis via Getty Images

**Is Mount Rushmore Next?:** National Park Service

**He Believed in America and its Anti-Slavery Document, the Constitution:** Wikipedia

**Explained Judaism's Moral Vision:** Joel Orent

**Moses of Her People:** Wikipedia

**Betsy Ross, Abolitionist and American Hero:** GraphicaArtis/Getty Images

**Holocaust Slave Labor, Then Death:** © Corbis/Corbis via Getty Images

**The Struggle for Civil Rights:** Afro American Newspapers/Gado/ Getty Images

# Image Credits

**Operation Magic Carpet:** Universal History Archive/Universal Images Group via Getty Images
**Rejoining the People of Israel:** Jenny Vaughan/AFP via Getty Images
**Visiting the Troops:** Bettmann/Getty Images

## Chapter Seven

**A Thinker's Thinker:** Terry Ashe/The LIFE Images Collection via Getty Images/Getty Images

## Chapter Eight

**No Honest Job was Demeaning:** Library of Congress archives
**The Sanctity of Study:** Dan Porges/Getty Images
**Hard Work Breeds Success:** HUD archives
**The Will to Succeed:** Emma McIntyre/Getty Images

## Chapter Nine

**Communist/Socialist Unity:** Jose Goitia/Gamma-Rapho via Getty Images
**Reagan and Begin - Two Principled Conservatives:** Israel Government Press Office
**An Economic and Strategic Peace Process:** Saul Loeb/AFP via Getty Images
**One Child Good, Two Child Bad:** Goh Chai Hin/AFP via Getty Images

## Chapter Ten

**Welcoming the Sabbath:** David Rubin
**Sabbath Peace in Israel:** Sharon Altshul
**Extending the Warmth of the Sabbath Day:** Sharon Altshul, with permission of Shlomo Katz

## Chapter Eleven

**The Cancel Culture Shuts Her Down:** Roberto Schmidt/AFP via Getty Images
**Raising New Young Radicals:** Wikipedia
**One Nation Under God:** © Hill Street Studios/Blend Images LLC via Getty Images

# Endnotes

## *Introduction*

(1) https://www.youtube.com/watch?v=4MJ8xiNHgA4

(2) https://en.wikipedia.org/wiki/Occupy_Wall_Street

(3) https://www.youtube.com/watch?v=rF4uBWFRCSE

(4) https://www.wusa9.com/article/news/local/vandalism-fires-dozens-of-arrests-in-dc-inauguration-protests/65-388634528

(5) https://www.washingtonexaminer.com/washington-secrets/powder-keg-61-say-us-on-verge-of-civil-war-52-already-prepping

(6) https://nypost.com/2021/01/06/neo-nazis-among-protesters-who-stormed-us-capitol/

https://www.theepochtimes.com/video-facts-matter-jan-15-blm-activist-who-stormed-capitol-is-charged-undercover-video-twitters-true-plan_3659430.html

https://www.politico.com/news/2021/01/14/liberal-activist-charged-capitol-riot-459553

## *Chapter One – The Israel-US Connection*

(1) https://www.jewishvirtuallibrary.org/u-s-presidential-quotes-about-jewish-homeland-and-israel-jewish-virtual-library

(2) Kook, Rabbi Avraham Yitzhak HaCohen. Arpilei Tohar. The Rabbi Tzvi Yehuda Kook Institute. Jerusalem, 1983.

(3) Epictetus, Sharon Lebell (2013). "The Art of Living: The Classical Manual on Virtue, Happiness, and Effectiveness", p.10, Harper Collins.

(4) Benson, Michael T. Harry S. Truman and the Founding of Israel. Praeger Publishers, 1997: 191.

(5) Ibid., 190.

(6) Ibid., 191.

(7) https://www.forbes.com/sites/davidadesnik/2014/08/06/jimmy-carter-calls-for-recognizing-hamas-legitimacy/#178f9b632c71

(8) http://www.telegraph.co.uk/news/worldnews/barackobama/7521220/Obama-snubbed-Netanyahu-for-dinnerwith-Michelle-and-the-girls-Israelis-claim.html

(9)  http://www.jpost.com/Arab-Israeli-Conflict/Leaked-documentclaims-UN-anti-settlement-resolution-orchestrated-by-US-PA-coop-476736

(10)  Helms, Jesse (January 11, 1995). "Jesse Helms: Setting the Record Straight". Middle East Quarterly (Interview). 2 (1). Interviewed by Daniel Pipes; Patrick Clawson. Middle East Forum. Retrieved 2018-06-01.

(11)  https://www.washingtonpost.com/local/trafficandcommuting/us-unveils-new-restrictions-on-travelers-from-eight-muslim-majority-countries/2017/03/21/d4efd080-0dcb-11e7-9d5a-a83e627dc120_story.html

(12)  https://ips-dc.org/why_the_us_supports_israel/

(13)  Frisch, Prof. Hillel. Myth: Israel Is the Largest Beneficiary of US Military Aid. BESA Center Perspectives Paper No. 410, February 10, 2017.

(14)  http://www.aproundtable.org/tps30info/beliefs.html

http://www.revolutionary-war-and-beyond.com/john-adamsquotations- 2.html

(15)  http://www.abrahamlincolnonline.org/lincoln/speeches/faithquotes.htm

## Chapter Two – Values of the American Republic

(1)  http://www.leaderu.com/orgs/cdf/onug/franklin.html

(2)  Katsh, Abraham. "The Biblical Heritage of American Democracy." (New York, 1977): 97.

(3)  https://www.britannica.com/topic/Founding-Fathers/The-achievement

(4)  Ibid.

(5)  https://www.britannica.com/topic/Founding-Fathers/The-explanations

(6)  https://www.britannica.com/topic/Founding-Fathers/The-achievement

(7)  https://www.nationalreview.com/2019/03/democrat-opposition-constitutional-order-electoral-college/

(8)  Ibid.

(9)  Ibid.

(10)  http://www.pewglobal.org/2010/12/02/muslims-around-the-world-divided-on-hamas-and-hezbollah/

(11) http://www.foundingfatherquotes.com/category/god

(12) https://www.thoughtco.com/republic-vs-democracy-4169936#the-concept-of-a-republic

(13) https://www.ushistory.org/declaration/document/

(14) https://www.britannica.com/topic/Founding-Fathers/The-achievement

(15) Federer, William. J. "What Every American Needs to Know About the Qur'an – A History of Islam & the United States." St. Louis: AmeriSearch Inc., Jan. 2007: 274.

(16) www.beitbresheet.com/Heritage/Heritage.htm

(17) https://en.wikipedia.org/wiki/Mandatory_Palestine

(18) https://mfa.gov.il/mfa/aboutisrael/history/pages/israels%20war%20of%20independence%20-%201947%20-%201949.aspx

(19) https://www.pewforum.org/2016/03/08/israels-religiously-divided-society/

(20) Ibid.

*Chapter Three – Domestic Terrorism is Not Social Justice*

(1) https://www.azquotes.com/author/37865-Socrates

(2) https://www.brainyquote.com/quotes/robert_kennedy_745981?src=t_mob

(3) https://en.wikipedia.org/wiki/George_Floyd

(4) https://www.bbc.com/news/world-us-canada-52905408

(5) https://www.cbsnews.com/news/michael-brown-ferguson-police-officer-no-charges-darren-wilson/

(6) https://www.foxnews.com/politics/new-squad-member-jamaal-bowman-renews-call-to-defund-the-police-after-tamir-rice-probe-results-in-no-charges

(7) https://www.bbc.com/news/world-us-canada-52905408

(8) https://www.marketwatch.com/story/more-police-officers-are-shot-and-killed-by-blacks-than-police-officers-kill-african-americans-claims-former-new-york-city-mayor-giuliani-2020-06-17

(9) https://www.npr.org/sections/live-updates-protests-for-racial-justice/2020/06/04/869278494/medical-examiners-autopsy-reveals-george-floyd-had-positive-test-for-coronavirus (10) https://www.nytimes.com/2020/06/03/us/leaders-activists-george-floyd-protests.html

(11) https://www.nbcnews.com/news/us-news/minneapolis-mayor-says-anger-over-george-floyd-death-not-only-n1216656

(12) https://www.foxnews.com/politics/biden-says-some-funding-should-absolutely-be-redirected-from-police

(13) https://www.huffpost.com/entry/minneapolis-mayor-jacob-frey-booed-abolish-police_n_5edc5396c5b64fc8dcbd87ce

(14) https://nypost.com/2020/06/08/rep-omar-dismantle-rotten-minneapolis-police-department/

(15) Kroman, David (June 5, 2020). "Seattle issues 30-day ban on tear gas at protests". Crosscut. Archived from the original on June 27, 2020. Retrieved June 28, 2020.

(16) "Seattle-area protests: Live updates for Sunday, June 7". The Seattle Times. June 7, 2020. Archived from the original on June 15, 2020. Retrieved June 17, 2020.

(17) https://www.usatoday.com/story/news/nation/2020/06/14/inside-seattle-autonomous-zone-black-protesters-seek-lasting-change/3179232001/

(18) https://www.thedailybeast.com/cheats/2016/08/01/blm-platform-calls-for-reparations

(19) https://www.politico.com/2020-election/candidates-views-on-the-issues/economy/reparations/

(20) https://www.wsj.com/articles/the-danger-of-debating-reparations-for-slavery-11556837452 and https://theconversation.com/american-slavery-separating-fact-from-myth-79620

*Chapter Four – Escalating Demands Amid Low-Level Warfare*

(1) https://www.brainyquote.com/authors/thomas-sowell-quotes

(2) https://www.brainyquote.com/quotes/christopher_hitchens_168002

(3) https://wfpl.org/cuban-community-rallies-behind-nulu-restaurant-after-controversy-over-blm-demands/

(4) Ibid.

(5) https://en.wikipedia.org/wiki/Shooting_of_David_Dorn

(6) https://www.kmov.com/news/second-man-charged-in-connection-with-death-of-retired-st-louis-police-captain-david-dorn/article_710c43a6-a90d-11ea-a7fb-773f3e096e33.html

(7) https://www.keepinspiring.me/martin-luther-king-jr-quotes/

(8) https://www.npr.org/sections/live-updates-protests-for-racial-justice/2020/07/01/886000386/de-blasio-on-shifting-1-billion-from-nypd-we-think-it-s-the-right-thing-to-do

(9) https://www.foxnews.com/us/new-york-city-police-cuomo-de-blasio-blue-lives-matter

(10) https://newyork.cbslocal.com/2020/07/16/power-of-prayer-march-brooklyn-bridge-protests-new-york-city-nypd-police-reform/

(11) https://www.foxnews.com/politics/kamala-harris-slammed-tweet-small-businesses-bailing-out-rioters

(12) https://thepostmillennial.com/portland-mayor-finally-denounces-antifa-following-explosive-clash-with-police

(13) https://apnews.com/96be8a461ab0f3886fc1723607c926e7

(14) https://www.foxnews.com/us/black-portland-police-sergeant-defund-police-concern

(15) https://www.detroitnews.com/story/news/local/detroit-city/2020/09/15/im-not-leaving-job-detroit-police-chief-james-craig/5801056002/

(16) https://nypost.com/2020/08/01/protestors-burn-bible-american-flag-as-tensions-rise-in-portland/

(17) Joan Peters. From Time Immemorial: The Origins of the Arab-Jewish Conflict over Palestine Harper & Row: New York, 1984.

(18) The Book of Joshua (The Bible).

(19) https://en.wikipedia.org/wiki/Jericho_bus_firebombing#:~:text=The%20Jericho%20bus%20firebombing%20was,the%20wounding%20of%205%20others.

(20) https://thetruthaboutrockthrowing.wordpress.com/the-victims/yehuda-shoham/

(21) https://www.merriam-webster.com/dictionary/riot

(22) https://dictionary.cambridge.org/dictionary/english/insurrection

(23) https://www.israelnationalnews.com/News/News.aspx/286641

(24) https://nypost.com/2020/09/09/the-ugly-privilege-of-rich-white-protesters/

(25) https://www.foxnews.com/us/wealthy-nyc-woman-20-facing-4-years-in-prison-after-blm-rampage

(26) https://en.wikipedia.org/wiki/Patty_Hearst

(27) https://www.curatedquotes.com/leadership-quotes/lincoln/

(28) https://www.foxnews.com/us/black-lives-matter-holds-rally-chicago-support-arrested-looting-unrest

(29) https://nypost.com/2019/07/22/total-anarchy-nypd-cops-get-drenched-by-buckets-of-water/

(30) https://www.foxnews.com/us/election-day-white-house-demonstrations-zoom-calls-shutdown-dc

## *Chapter Five – Appeasement Does Not Work*

(1) https://www.brainyquote.com/quotes/winston_churchill_100130

(2) https://www.goodreads.com/quotes/tag/freedom

(3) https://en.wikipedia.org/wiki/Munich_Agreement

(4) http://www.mfa.gov.il/MFA/Peace+Process/Guide+to+the+Peace+Process/THE+ISRAELI-PALESTINIAN+INTERIM+AGREEMENT.htm

(5) https://www.wsj.com/articles/abbas-we-welcome-every-drop-of-blood-spilled-in-jerusalem-1445209820

(6) https://www.nytimes.com/1994/05/20/world/rabin-says-arafat-s-jihad-remark-set-back-peace-effort.html

(7) https://www.jpost.com/arab-israeli-conflict/pa-must-halt-pay-for-slay-policy-for-peace-and-prosperity-analysis-616521

(8) http://www.israelnationalnews.com/News/News.aspx/139574

(9) https://en.wikipedia.org/wiki/Tomorrow%27s_Pioneers

(10) https://tennesseestar.com/2019/12/27/semester-of-violence-physical-attacks-on-conservative-college-students-keep-piling-up/

(11) https://www.nationalreview.com/corner/just-how-liberal-are-college-professors/

(12) https://www.teachingforblacklives.org/read-the-introduction

(13) Ibid.

(14) https://www.foxnews.com/media/buffalo-public-school-

teaching-elementary-students-to-question-nuclear-family-as-part-of-blm-integrated-curriculum-tucker

(15) https://freebeacon.com/culture/tony-baltimore-school-buckles-to-anti-semitic-demands-of-black-lives-matter-activists/

(16) Ibid.

(17) https://www.thejewishstar.com/stories/alignment-of-bds-and-blm-poses-growing-threat-to-jews-in-israel-and-the-diaspora,19540

(18) https://www.youtube.com/watch?v=4TJK1a8OHyw

(19) Horowitz, David. "Barack Obama's Rules For Revolution: The Alinsky Model." David Horowitz Freedom Center. Sherman Oaks, CA, 2009.

(20) Ibid.

(21) https://www.youtube.com/watch?v=h95xndYNb4s

(22) Ibid.

(23) Horowitz, David. "Barack Obama's Rules For Revolution: The Alinsky Model." David Horowitz Freedom Center. Sherman Oaks, CA, 2009.

## *Chapter Six – History Matters*

(1) https://www.jewishvirtuallibrary.org/myths-and-facts-quotes

(2) https://www.goodreads.com/work/quotes/153313-nineteen-eighty-four

(3) Orwell, George. Nineteen Eighty-Four [1984], Secker & Warburg, London, 1949.

(4) https://www.sfchronicle.com/bayarea/philmatier/article/SF-may-erase-presidents-names-from-schools-15433452.php

(5) https://denverite.com/2020/06/23/what-other-places-and-buildings-in-denver-are-primed-for-a-name-change-the-citys-looking-into-that/

(6) https://www.fi.edu/benjamin-franklin/famous-quotes

(7) Frederick Douglass (1855). The Anti-Slavery Movement, A Lecture by Frederick Douglass before the Rochester Ladies' Anti-Slavery Society. Press of Lee, Mann & Company, Daily American Office. p. 33.

(8) https://www.fi.edu/benjamin-franklin/famous-quotes.

(9) Soloveitchik, Rabbi Joseph B. "Reflections of the Rav." Besdin, Abraham ed. Jerusalem, Publishing Department of the Jewish Agency, Chapter 2.

(10) https://www.foxnews.com/opinion/cabot-phillips-cancel-culture-distorts-history-to-portray-us-as-evil-nation-that-must-be-transformed

(11) https://www.forbes.com/sites/tomlindsay/2019/08/30/after-all-didnt-america-invent-slavery/#3d2915dd7ef6

(12) https://www.nytimes.com/2019/07/02/business/betsy-ross-shoe-kaepernick-nike.html

(13) https://www.forbes.com/sites/tomlindsay/2019/08/30/after-all-didnt-america-invent-slavery/#3d2915dd7ef6

(14) Kook, Rabbi Avraham Yitzhak. "Orot HaTeshuva" (Lights of Penitence). Kook, Rabbi Tzvi Yehuda ed. Or Etzion, 1991. (Originally published 1925).

(15) https://www.haaretz.com/israel-news/.premium.MAGAZINE-the-yemenite-immigrants-who-rebelled-against-the-new-israeli-state-1.5453410

(16) https://en.wikipedia.org/wiki/Aliyah_from_Ethiopia

(17) Kook, Rabbi Tzvi Yehuda. "Mitoch HaTorah Hagoelet" (Within the Redeeming Torah). Avihu Schwartz ed. Jerusalem 1983.

(18) https://chrisstevensonauthor.com/2017/04/14/washingtons-self-sacrifice-a-message-kids-need-to-hear/

(19) https://www.linkedin.com/pulse/sacrifices-george-washington-why-still-matter-today-nik-d-agostino

(20) Ibid.

(21) http://en.wikipedia.org/wiki/Haym_Solomon

(22) https://www.linkedin.com/pulse/sacrifices-george-washington-why-still-matter-today-nik-d-agostino

(23) Ibid.

*Chapter Seven – Changing Semantics Ignoring Facts*

(1) https://www.google.com/search?q=semantics+quotes&sxsrf=ALeKk00qZNzCekzLVMvaK6K01gh-8w9gsw:15988936
14572&tbm=isch&source=iu&ictx=1&fir=uCe7V0r9CfVB
eM%252CMYRjeNzln3cQbM%252C_&vet=1&usg=AI4_-
kQmamCtazgMilnLFwrMFzjX-OVj6Q&sa=X&ved=2ahU

KEwiPlbjv9sXrAhXOUMAKHXM6AUQQ9QF6BAgJED
Q&biw=1506&bih=690#imgrc=Sq_NXU1vHwfUmM

(2) Ibid.

(3) Foreign Relations Authorization, Fiscal Years 1986 and 1987: Hearings Before ... By United States. Congress. Senate. Committee on Foreign Relations.

(4) Ibid.

(5) https://www.jewishvirtuallibrary.org/origin-of-quot-palestine-quot

(6) https://www.merriam-webster.com/dictionary/liberate

(7) https://milog.co.il/%D7%A4%D7%9C%D7%A9

(8) https://www.merriam-webster.com/dictionary/settler

(9) https://besacenter.org/perspectives-papers/palestinians-settlers-colonialism/

(10) https://thefederalist.com/2018/05/01/lefts-war-words-manipulates-mind/

(11) https://www.merriam-webster.com/dictionary/liberal

(12) https://www.merriam-webster.com/dictionary/progressive

(13) https://www.washingtontimes.com/news/2021/jan/2/no-more-he-she-father-mother-new-house-rules-go-ge/

(14) https://www.usatoday.com/story/life/tv/2016/08/22/gmas-amy-robach-says-on-air-racial-slur-a-mistake/89108496/

(15) https://news.gallup.com/poll/268766/socialism-popular-capitalism-among-young-adults.aspx

(16) https://www.sparknotes.com/lit/1984/quotes/theme/mind-control/

(17) https://www.sparknotes.com/lit/1984/context/historical/why-orwell-wrote-1984/#:~:text=While%20fighting%20in%20the%20Spanish,the%20political%20satire%20of%201984

(18) Ibid.

*Chapter Eight – Family, Education, and Hard Work Matter*

(1) https://www.brainyquote.com/authors/daniel-patrick-moynihan-quotes

(2) https://nypost.com/2005/04/16/mayor-takes-slap-at-jew-baiter-fulani/

(3) https://www.counterpunch.org/2020/07/29/black-lives-matter-and-the-nuclear-family/

(4) https://front.moveon.org/moveons-electoral-work/

(5) https://www.counterpunch.org/2020/07/29/black-lives-matter-and-the-nuclear-family/

(6) https://www.vox.com/the-highlight/2019/5/20/185 42843/intersectionality-conservatism-law-race-gender-discrimination

(7) https://www.chabad.org/library/article_cdo/aid/558598/jewish/Does-Jewish-Law-Forbid-Polygamy.htm

(8) Louis Greenberg, The Jews in Russia (New York: Shocken Books, 1976).

(9) https://www.ynetnews.com/articles/0,7340,L-4099803,00.html

(10) Ibid.

(11) Ibid.

(12) Ibid.

(13) https://mishpacha.com/words-not-heard/

(14) https://en.wikipedia.org/wiki/Ben_Carson

(15) https://en.wikipedia.org/wiki/Oprah_Winfrey

(16) https://www.gatestoneinstitute.org/8956/black-lives-matter-antisemitism

(17) Seymour Martin Lipset, "The Socialism of Fools – The Left, the Jews and Israel," Encounter, (December 1969), p. 24.

## Chapter Nine – Did Israeli Socialism Work?

(1) https://www.geckoandfly.com/25752/anti-socialism-quotes-medical-healthcare-tax/

(2) Ibid.

(3) Ibid.

(4) https://news.gallup.com/poll/240725/democrats-positive-socialism-capitalism.aspx

(5) https://www.commdiginews.com/politics-2/george-soros-gave-black-lives-matter-and-antifa-over-100-million-dollars-130048/

(6) https://www.israelhayom.com/opinions/sanitizing-soros-through-guilt-by-association/

(7) https://www.foxnews.com/opinion/tucker-carlson-george-soros-george-gascon-los-angeles

(8) https://boulderjewishnews.org/2012/shopping-the-rich-jewish-history-of-department-stores/ and https://en.wikipedia.org/wiki/List_of_Jewish_American_businesspeople_in_retail

(9) https://www.jewishvirtuallibrary.org/prominent-companies-founded-by-jews-in-america

(10) https://mosaicmagazine.com/picks/israel-zionism/2015/02/the-root-of-israels-economic-woes-isnt-the-settlements-its-socialism/?print

(11) https://www.nationalreview.com/2019/10/failure-of-socialism-israel-india-united-kingdom-adopted-free-market-policies-and-prospered/

(12) Ibid.

(13) Ibid.

(14) Ibid.

(15) https://www.jewishpress.com/blogs/the-lid-jeffdunetz/when-begin-eviscerated-biden-for-threatening-him/2019/04/30/

(16) https://www.nationalreview.com/2019/10/failure-of-socialism-israel-india-united-kingdom-adopted-free-market-policies-and-prospered/

(17) https://theculturetrip.com/middle-east/israel/articles/11-israeli-innovations-that-changed-the-world/

(18) https://seekingalpha.com/article/4151094-how-israel-became-startup-nation-3rd-companies-on-nasdaq

(19) https://www.ft.com/content/01e0cdcc-09fd-11df-8b23-00144feabdc0

### Chapter Ten – Finding Tranquility Amidst the Chaos

(1) Heschel, Abraham Joshua. "The Sabbath, Its Meaning for Modern Man". The Noonday Press, 1994.

(2) https://www.brainyquote.com/quotes/joyce_giraud_654411

(3) https://courses.lumenlearning.com/boundless-sociology/chapter/the-conflict-perspective-on-religion/

(4) Ibid.

(5) https://www.newsobserver.com/news/coronavirus/article243468536.html

(6) https://www.vox.com/the-goods/2020/3/26/21193038/ millennials-moving-home-coronavirus-pandemic

(7) https://www.latimes.com/california/story/2020-04-11/ coronavirus-milennial-parents-roommates-isolation

(8) https://jamanetwork.com/journals/jamapediatrics/ fullarticle/485781

(9) https://www.fatherly.com/health-science/6-reasons-eating-family-dinner/

(10) https://www.parents.com/recipes/tips/unexpected-benefits-of-eating-together-as-a-family-according-to-science/

(11) https://www.timesofisrael.com/ivanka-trump-happy-to-be-jewish/

(12) Kaplan, Aryeh. "Sabbath Day of Eternity". Orthodox Union/NCSY, 1974.

(13) Ibid.

(14) Rubin, David. "Trump and the Jews". Jerusalem, 2018.

(15) https://en.wikipedia.org/wiki/Blue_laws_in_the_United_ States and https://www.sabbathtruth.com/free-resources/ article-library/id/1840/what-are-blue-laws

### Chapter Eleven – Confronting the Revolution

(1) Orwell, George. "Animal Farm". Harcourt, Brace, and Co: London, UK, 1946.

(2) https://www.sparknotes.com/lit/animalfarm/section10/

(3) https://www.history.com/topics/germany/weimar-republic

(4) https://www.foxnews.com/us/subway-shovings-flamethrowers-nyc-descends-into-anarchy

(5) https://www.foxnews.com/us/protesters-raid-shops-atms-following-police-shooting-of-philadelphia-man
https://www.foxnews.com/us/walter-wallace-philadelphia-police-rap-cops
https://www.foxnews.com/us/night-two-of-philadelphia-unrest-begins-as-wallaces-kids-speak-out

(6) https://nypost.com/2020/10/29/blm-mob-violently-chases-jewish-men-at-philadelphia-protest/

(7) http://www.israelnationalnews.com/News/News. aspx/291362

(8) http://www.israelnationalnews.com/News/News.aspx/291233

(9) https://www.foxnews.com/politics/trump-supporters-hit-with-fireworks-at-restaurant-after-maga-march-suspect-arrested

(10) https://www.foxnews.com/media/kelley-paul-says-dc-violence-of-trump-supporters-brings-back-awful-memories-calls-out-media-bias

(11) https://www.foxnews.com/politics/rand-paul-dc-us-attorney-wont-investigate-protestors-who-confronted-him-at-rnc

(12) https://nypost.com/2021/01/06/neo-nazis-among-protesters-who-stormed-us-capitol/

https://www.theepochtimes.com/video-facts-matter-jan-15-blm-activist-who-stormed-capitol-is-charged-undercover-video-twitters-true-plan_3659430.html

https://www.politico.com/news/2021/01/14/liberal-activist-charged-capitol-riot-459553

(13) https://www.newsbreak.com/district-of-columbia/washington/news/1583520112758/george-soros-gave-black-lives-matter-and-antifa-over-100-million-dollars

(14) https://builtin.com/diversity-inclusion/companies-that-support-black-lives-matter-social-justice

(15) https://www.hollywoodintoto.com/stars-fund-protesters-not-victims/

(16) https://www.wsj.com/articles/SB122212856075765367

(17) https://www.brainyquote.com/quotes/martin_luther_king_jr_115056

(18) https://besacenter.org/perspectives-papers/twitter-trump-khamenei/

https://www.foxnews.com/opinion/trump-twitter-facebook-patrice-onwuka

(19) https://imprimis.hillsdale.edu/orwells-1984-today/?fbclid=IwAR0bKdo7rlXHPwvT6wnvwgH3wHpuNB1oTxdIMfpmfad2T1nyEFhiJueMkcI

(20) https://www.kctv5.com/news/local_news/hawley-book-cancellation-could-not-be-more-orwellian/article_41bb1ada-19c5-58ff-bcae-a2993d2c98eb.html

# Other Books By David Rubin

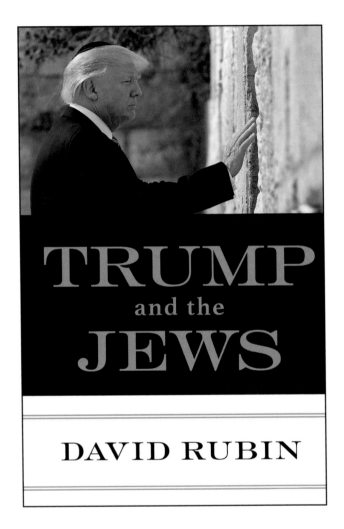

**Trump and the Jews**
ISBN: 978-0-9829067-7-4

Available online at www.DavidRubinIsrael.com/books/
~ Phone orders 1-800-431-1579 ~ Or at a bookstore near you!

**Peace For Peace**
**Israel In The New Middle East**
ISBN: 978-0-9829067-4-3

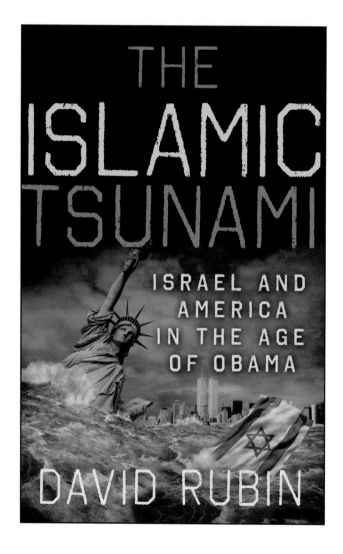

Available online at www.DavidRubinIsrael.com/books/
~ Phone orders 1-800-431-1579 ~ Or at a bookstore near you!

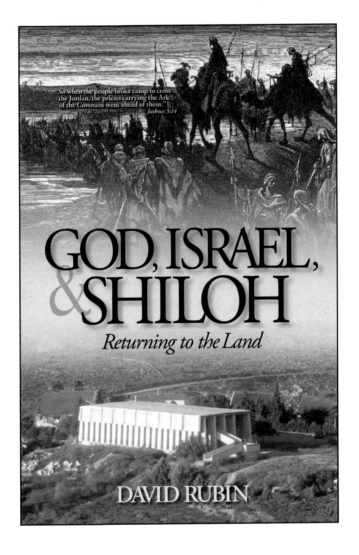

**God, Israel, & Shiloh**
**Returning to the Land**
ISBN: 978-0-9829067-2-9